A Single Parent's Survival Guide

Other Books by Dr. Leroy Baruth published by Kendall/Hunt Publishing Co.:

ABC'S OF CLASSROOM DISCIPLINE
   (with Dan Eckstein)

LIFE STYLE: THEORY, PRACTICE AND RESEARCH
   (with Dan Eckstein)

LIFE STYLE: WHAT IT IS AND HOW TO DO IT
   (with Dan Eckstein and Dave Mahrer)

A Single Parent's Survival Guide

How to Raise the Children

Leroy G. Baruth

University of South Carolina

KENDALL/HUNT PUBLISHING COMPANY

2460 Kerper Boulevard,
Dubuque, Iowa 52001

Copyright © 1979 by Kendall/Hunt Publishing Company

Library of Congress Catalog Card Number: 79-2388

ISBN 0-8403-2053-1

Printed in the United States of America

B   402053   01

With love to my daughters, Seana, Kelly and Katey, who have provided me with ample opportunity to utilize the techniques presented in this book.

Contents

Preface

This book is based on the belief that children raised in a single parent family can be as happy and well adjusted as children in two parent families. The concept that a single parent family is a "broken home" rather than an alternate family system and that the children cannot be well adjusted is totally inaccurate. The important factor is that a healthy relationship exists between parent and children.

The child rearing principles presented are based on the work of Alfred Adler and Rudolf Dreikurs. This approach is particularly appropriate for single parent families because there is a joint sharing of decision making and responsibility. Many times the single parent feels alone and frustrated; however, by getting the entire family involved, these feelings can be greatly alleviated.

Child rearing techniques such as encouragement, consequences, and the family council are discussed. Numerous examples are cited to demonstrate how these techniques can be used in coping with some of the particular problems of single parents and also some situations that are of concern in two parent families as well.

I believe that you will find this book extremely helpful not only in learning how to cope with your children's misbehavior, but also in developing a very positive, supportive relationship with your children.

Leroy G. Baruth

Acknowledgments

I would like to express my grateful appreciation to the following:

Albino Hinojosa for his illustrations that added to the understanding and readability of the material presented;

James Reynolds, Associate Editor of Kendall/Hunt Publishing Company, for his confidence, support and encouragement;

Ruth Smith and Carolyn Cheek who provided background material related to single parent families;

Ken Marlin and Practical Parenting Publications for permission to reprint *The Basics of Practical Parenting;*

The Oregon State University Extension Service for permission to reprint *The Family Council* by Thomas Poffenberger;

Houghton Mifflin Company for permission to reprint material from *The Great Santini* by Pat Conroy;

The Rudolf Dreikurs Unit of the Family Education Association, Chicago, for permission to reprint *The ABC's of Guiding the Child;* and

Ann Parks, Information Center of Parents Without Partners, Inc., for permission to reprint the annotated bibliographies related to single parenthood.

1
You Are Not Alone

As a single parent you may feel that your situation is unique. Well, in the United States there are millions of families headed by a single parent. Approximately ninety percent of these families are headed by women and the other ten percent by men. This book is designed to provide suggestions to help you as a single parent, in raising your children.

Before we start let's examine some types of single parent families. There are six basic types of single parents: widowed, divorced, separated, never married, adopting parent and those separated for an extended period such as for military duty. The problems single parents face initially are often related to the event that led to their current status. As time goes on, however, their problems become more similar, not only to other single parents, but to two parent families as well.

The Widowed Parent

After the death of a spouse, the family frequently experiences an acute sense of loss and disorientation. They have a great deal of readjusting to do in terms of the financial, social, and emotional problems which are thrust upon them by the loss of one parent, particularly if the parent is the father.

Quite often the widow is unprepared for sudden death, as are her children. A period of grief and mourning is followed by the realistic fact that she is now a one parent head of the family with economic and social changes which may seem frightening. Loneliness will probably emerge as her single most dominant characteristic. Specifically, she may miss the partnership in the many perplexities of child-rearing which can normally be dealt with more securely through joint rather than single responsibility.

To make the situation more complex, the children are likely to hold a fear of losing the second parent. They think "one parent has left me. How do I know my mother won't leave me too?" The world of the child has been shaken and has become less secure. Open discussion of this fear and reassurance help, but time and experience are the best cures. It takes a while to learn again that mother can go away and will come back and that her leaving is not another desertion.

The children may also express anger toward the deceased parent. If the parent had a prolonged illness which deprived the children of the other parent's attention, the child may say "I'm glad he's gone." Or the children may be angry with their new life and their "different" status and blame the deceased parent.

One final consideration which is certainly evident to the parent and frequently evident to the children is the change in financial status. This family unit can only hope that the father provided an adequate will or life insurance policy as a means of supplementing the household income. Unlike the divorced parent, no monthly check can be hoped for otherwise. In most cases, the mother must go to work, whether she had been working previously or not.

The Divorced Parent

This type of single parent family shares many of the same problems of the bereaved family, in that divorce is a death of a kind. The difference is that this situation many times lacks closure and, unfortunately, the children may vainly hope that some day mom and dad will be together again and "everything will be all right."

In most cases of divorce there has been adequate warning or even preparation that a one parent family will develop. During the waiting period there may be a separation and children are frequently involved in the quarrels, discriminations, and accusations of the parents. The single parent and the children are likely to experience the same four emotions as the bereaved family: frustration, failure, guilt, and ambivalence. However, these may be in a somewhat different vein since the way in which they arrived in the situation differs.

The divorced parents' sense of frustration may come from their confusion about the new status in society, their loneliness and fears, and their resentment about not being able to "walk away from it all." Both children and parent are desirous of ending the state of incompleteness that frustrates them. This is why children often will encourage their single parent to remarry and regain the sense of completeness (possibly before the parent is psychologically ready to remarry).

The breakup of a marriage is frequently viewed as a personal failure by both the single parent and the children. The parent's feelings often center around the original selection of the marriage partner. For the children, the sense of failure seems to relate to their inability to prevent the family breakup. Doubts about personal worth are likely to be expressed by these children.

Besides the guilt resulting from the perceived failure, single parents often feel new guilt from feeling that the children's needs might have been neglected. The children's guilt might stem from their perception that they are the cause of the deterioration of the marriage.

The single parent may feel ambivalent about the children depending on the current mood. If mother is tired after a long day, she may feel shackled and resentful about the presence of her children. If things are going well in mother's life, she may feel privileged to share in the experiences of her children.

After the separation and divorce, the children face difficulties such as the question of visitation, dual loyalties, and frequently two families if the other parent remarries. Financial arrangements between the parents frequently cause intense conflict and most often the problems center on the children. The parent with custody often feels burdened by the primary responsibility for the children and resents the apparent freedom of the other parent. Eventually, even in middle income families, child support becomes a problem and the parents tend to "bargain" with the child visitation rights.

The Separated Parent

Many of the considerations that apply to divorced parents apply to separated parents, but there are some noteworthy exceptions. The separated woman finds herself in a vacuum as far as our society is concerned. In her social life, most separated mothers feel uncomfortable because they are neither single, nor married, and not legally free to marry again.

The children are usually unprepared for the separation when it occurs. Although they are almost always aware of a strain at home, most parents fail to explain the separation to the children before it happens. It is understandable, then, that most children are negatively affected by the separation. It is difficult to handle questions and attitudes about the absent parent and this can cause children to have trouble in school and to experience health problems. Many of these children feel humiliated at being abandoned by their parent. The fact that most children do not know the reason for the separation adds to their anxieties and they become embarrassed when asked about their absent parent.

The Never Married Parent

An ever increasing number of unmarried mothers are deciding to keep their children. In the past society has tended to reject these parents, however this trend seems to be changing. More middle class unmarried women deliberately become pregnant, often without even letting the man know he was the father. Others accidently conceive and decide to go through with the pregnancy even though marriage with the baby's father is not likely.

The problems of the unmarried mothers are greater than those of widows and divorcees. For them, there is no widow's pension or alimony payments. The same financial considerations that plague all single parent families are even more severe for the majority of these women.

In recent years there has been increasing interest in counseling and helping unmarried fathers. Often engulfed with guilt feelings and unsure of their responsibilities, these men seek help. Their role still is very ill defined.

Children of an unmarried mother typically do not miss their father in the way other children do because many times they do not know their father. As the child grows older, an increasing interest in the father and his whereabouts is common. As in the case of the divorced parent and separated parent, the mother does well not to belittle the father.

The Adopting Parent

In recent years single parents have been joined by a small but growing number who have freely chosen this role. Some single persons decide to adopt children. In the past, single parents were chosen only for youngsters no one else wanted. Today, however, single adults are actually sought out for many children. In cases involving older children particularly, there may be a better emotional relationship with just one parent. These children usually do not know their biological parents and are often curious about these ties.

Adopting parents are usually highly motivated to be good parents and provide well for their children. Unlike the situations in the widowed, divorced, or separated homes, this new situation is usually viewed as a welcome relief to the child who has often been in a children's home for several years.

The Parent Separated for an Extended Period

Very little material is written on the problems of the parent separated for an extended period, but they are similar in many ways to the other single parents, with one major exception; they usually do not suffer under the same financial worries.

In *The Great Santini,* Pat Conroy describes the anticipated return of the father and some of the problems of separation and the changing of authority upon his return:

> But Ben had watched his mother change as the day approached for his father to return from his year's journey overseas. It was a universal law in military families that mothers could not maintain the strict discipline enforced by fathers to whom discipline was a religion and a way of life. When the military man left for a year, the whole family relaxed in a collective, yet unvoiced sigh. For a year, there was a looseness, a freedom from tension, a time when martial law was suspended. Though a manless house was an uncompleted home, and though the father was keenly missed, there was a laxity and fragile vigor that could not survive his homecoming.
> Lillian Meecham (the mother) was not a disciplinarian, but as the day of her husband's return neared, she knew instinctively that she had to harden into a vestigial imitation of her husband, so his arrival would not be too much of a shock to her children. His hand had traditionally been very heavy when he returned from overseas, so intent was he on re-establishing codes of discipline and ensuring that the children marched to his harsher cadences. For the last month she had been preparing them. She conducted unannounced inspections, yelled frequently, scolded often, and had even slapped Matthew when he ar-

gued about one of her directives. Tension flowed like a black-water creek through the family as the day of Colonel Meecham's arrival neared. The change of command ceremony took place the moment his plane arrived at Smyther Field. Lillian Meecham would hand the household over to her husband without a single word passing between them.[1]

In a parent's absence and in their return, the family goes through some serious readjustments.

Before discussing some specific techniques to be used by single parents in child rearing there are some basic suggestions that might be appropriate at this time:

1. Be honest with your children about the situation that caused you to become a single parent. This should only be done to the extent that the children can understand and every effort should be made to present your spouse in a favorable light. Nothing is to be gained by making disparaging remarks about your former spouse.
2. If the situation involves a separation or divorce, assure the children that they are not responsible for the decision to discontinue the relationship.
3. Be honest about your own feelings. This will demonstrate to the children that it is all right for them to express how they feel. It is important, however, that after feelings have been expressed that constructive action be taken to begin coping with the situation. You should realize that feelings of anger, anxiety, and fear are frequent reactions to the situation. However, if such feelings persist for an extended period of time, professional help should be sought.
4. Try to maintain as much of the same routine and surroundings as possible. This will provide the children with a feeling of security that not everything has changed.
5. Do not try to be both mother and father to your children. Establish a family atmosphere of team work where responsibilities are shared.
6. In the case of separation or divorce, realize that the relationship is over and do not encourage the children to hope for a reconciliation.
7. The children must be reassured that they will continue to be loved, cared for, and supported. This should be done not only by words but also by your attitude and behavior.
8. You should not use the children in an effort to gain bargaining power with your separated or divorced spouse. Differences should be settled privately between the parents or in court.

1. Reprinted from *The Great Santini* by Pat Conroy, Copyright © 1976 by Pat Conroy. Used by permission of Houghton Mifflin Company.

9. Make use of grandparents and other relatives so the children maintain a sense of belonging to a continuing family.
10. Try to seek the companionship and counsel of other single parents. They can be a source of advice and support that will help immeasurably in child rearing. Many churches and communities have organizations for the single parent and, of course, Parents Without Partners Chapters are available nationwide.

Important Concepts

You are not alone! There are millions of other single parents in a situation similar to yours.

Child rearing in six types of single parent families will be discussed in this book.

Problems initially faced by single parents are often related to the event that led to their current status; however, their problems become more similar, not only to other single parent families, but to two parent families as well.

2
Understanding Your Children

There are many contemporary theories to explain why children behave the way they do. Some of these theories state that heredity is the most important factor; other theories maintain that the home environment is the primary influence. The child rearing approach discussed in this book advocates the desire to belong as a key concept in understanding children. Each child strives to find and maintain a place of significance in life.

The Family Constellation

One of the most influential factors to be considered in understanding children is the family constellation, the order of birth of children living within the single parent family and the dynamic relationship between siblings and other members of the family group. Driekurs, Grumwald and Pepper (1971) state that in the life-pattern of every person, "there is the imprint of his position in the family with its definite characteristics. It is upon this one fact— the child's subjective impression of his place in the family constellation—that much of his future attitude toward life depends (p. 46)." Therefore, we can see that to understand our children we must look at how they perceive their place in the family constellation.

A central concept to remember in learning about family constellation is that from the moment of birth the child acts in a way which he or she hopes to achieve significance or superiority in the family. Actions that are not productive in achieving these goals will be discarded and replaced by new behaviors aimed at the same goals.

Important Factors

When considering the family constellation, the age and sex of each sibling is extremely important because an unbalanced sibling sex distribution may cause special consideration. For example, a boy with four sisters would probably have a different outlook on life than a boy with four brothers.

Another important factor to consider is the age difference between siblings. Competition can be extremely keen between siblings that are close in age. This is especially true with a younger female who developmentally may "surpass" a slightly older brother. Conversely, siblings separated by several years may feel little, if any, competition. If the age difference is five or more years, the siblings are generally considered to be in two different sub-families.

Because of competition, usually the first and third siblings in a family have more in common than the first and second. This is because the oldest child will find a place in the family (i.e., the good student, the athlete, the social butterfly, or the artist) and the second sibling will usually select another area to excel. Usually this results from the oldest sibling having a head start and the difficulty the second sibling has in catching up and achieving the same level of competence. The third sibling usually differs from the second and thus tends to be much like the first.

When one sibling is physically or mentally handicapped, the other siblings are usually affected. They may be required to assume many of the responsibilities that would normally be carried out by the handicapped sibling or the single parent may have to devote more time to the care of the handicapped child and therefore may not have enough time to spend with the other siblings.

A difficult situation arises when one of the siblings dies during childhood. Normally the single parent will tend to be over-protective of the other siblings. Parents may also tend to compare the remaining siblings with the deceased child, by statements like, "Why aren't you as smart as your sister was?" or, "I wish you were more like Johnny used to be." This is an extremely difficult situation because a child cannot compete with a sibling who, in the parent's eyes, is approaching sainthood. It's difficult enough to compete with "mortal" siblings, but "angels in heaven" are untouchable.

When a half-brother or sister, cousins, or other children live with the family for an extended period of time, they become part of the family constellation. Usually the children will align themselves pretty much by age rather than the blood relationship to each other. This can be a traumatic experience for a child who has become accustomed to a particular place in the family constellation (especially oldest or youngest) and all of a sudden another child has that place. This is especially common when two single parents marry and can be referred to as the "Brady Bunch" syndrome.

Sibling Characteristics

There are certain characteristics that are common to each of the sibling positions within the family constellation; however, these characteristics represent a composite, so not every detail will apply in all cases. Eckstein, Baruth, and Mahrer (1978) describe some general characteristics of various ordinal positions:

Oldest Child: The oldest child has a unique situation in a family. Being born first entitles such a child to the parent's undivided attention, at least until another sibling is born. Usually an oldest child will conform to the parent's standards because he or she doesn't want to lose their favor. Such children tend to be very responsible because of their desire to meet the adult standards of their parents. When another sibling is born they often initially feel "dethroned." Usually because they are bigger and more capable, the threat of the new arrival will diminish with the passing of time. However, if the second child is very close in age to the first, there is a chance that the second might be more capable than the older. The situation of the second sibling permanently dethroning the first is most frequent when the older child is a boy followed very closely by a girl. Her accelerated rate of human growth and development makes such a "dethronement" more likely. Other frequent characteristics include preference for authority, dislike for change, conservative viewpoint, being "pacemaker" for the other children, ambitious, achievement oriented, and having a tendency to relate better to adults than peers.

Middle Child: The middle child will usually try to over-take the first as a result of what has become known as the "Avis Complex" (because I'm second I'll try harder). Usually the middle child will choose to compete in areas in which the oldest child is not proficient. If oldest children are good students, athletes, or models of good behavior, then middle children will probably be poor students, uninterested in athletics, and discipline problems; however, they might be good musicians, artists, or strong in an area where the oldest is not skilled. Whereas the oldest child is the "center of the universe" the second child must "slip in on the second act." Middle children tend to be more sociable than oldest children. They also are often sensitive to injustices, unfairness, feelings of being slighted or abused, or of having no place in the group. When a younger sibling is born into the family, the middle child often feels dethroned, because of the new competition from the youngest child.

Youngest Child: Youngest children have something going for them that the oldest, and middle children do not—they have never been dethroned. They are generally the most powerful persons in the family because of the many ways of getting the parents and other siblings to do things for them. Youngest children frequently are not taken seriously because they are the smallest, and as a result, they may be spoiled by others. Along with the oldest child, the youngest has a unique place in the family constellation. However, it should also be noted that youngest children should have good sibling models from which to observe and learn.

Single Child: Single children usually develop in one of two basic directions: either they will try to meet the adult level of competence or they will remain helpless and irresponsible as long as possible. Usually single children will have better relationships with people much older or much younger than they are, rather than with their peer group. Single children may refuse to cooperate when their every wish is not granted. They are similar to youngest children in that neither have ever been displaced. Single children are often loners, not very "sharing" oriented and may expect a "special place" without having to earn it.

In large families there can be several sub-families. It is not uncommon for several siblings to be considered first children in a large family if they are separated by more than five years. Large families are frequently characterized by less-competition among the middle siblings. The single parent usually has less time to spend with each sibling, so there is often very little for which the siblings can compete.

Family Atmosphere

The children first seek to find what they need to do to belong or be accepted in their initial social group—the family. If the single parent gives recognition and approval to those siblings who work hard, get good grades, or are sensitive to others, then the chances are that the children will strive toward preserving these characteristics. On the other hand if the single parent demonstrates characteristics like bitterness, resentfulness, or dishonesty then their children may well acquire these characteristics. In other words the parent sets the tone for demonstrating what is important.

Family values often account for similarities among children. If the parent is intellectual, creative, athletic or musical, then these abilities may become family values. The family standards or values do not determine the child's behavior; however, children of the same family usually lean toward similar behavior and develop values and morals accepted by the parent. In some situations the children are influenced in an opposite direction and adopt values and morals that are in direct contradiction to the rest of the family. This is usually viewed as a form of rebellion.

The important point to remember with regard to family constellation is that you, as a single parent, will be the primary influence on the values, behaviors and beliefs that your children acquire. The things that you model and accept will tend to be continued. The following quotation (Dreikurs and Cassell, 1972) illustrates the importance of family atmosphere:

If a child lives with criticism, he learns to condemn.
If a child lives with hostility, he learns to fight.
If a child lives with ridicule, he learns to be shy.
If a child lives with fear, he learns to be apprehensive.
If a child lives with shame, he learns to feel guilty.
If a child lives with tolerance, he learns to be patient.
If a child lives with encouragement, he learns to be confident.
If a child lives with acceptance, he learns to love.
If a child lives with recognition, he learns it is good to have a goal.
If a child lives with honesty, he learns what truth is.
If a child lives with fairness, he learns justice.
If a child lives with security, he learns to have faith in himself and those about him.
If a child lives with friendliness, he learns the world is a nice place in which to live, to love, and be loved (pp. 28–29).

Mistaken Goals

In order to understand children it is important to realize that all misbehavior is the result of a child's mistaken notion about the way to belong and be accepted. To deal more effectively with the child, the parent must first be able to recognize the child's mistaken goal. Rudolf Dreikurs (1968) has classified the goals of misbehavior as: (1) to gain attention, (2) to demonstrate power, (3) to punish or get even, and (4) to demonstrate inadequacy. These goals remain present in the behavior of older children and adults, but additional purposes can influence behavior as an individual matures.

Attention

Children whose mistaken goal is attention generally feel that they only belong when others notice them or when others are doing things for them. The parent usually feels annoyed and tends to remind and coax the child. In cases where the mistaken goal is attention the child will temporarily stop the behavior when reprimanded. Why? Because the child got attention. When the child again feels the need to be noticed, the same or a similar behavior will occur again. A point to remember is that all of us need to be recognized and noticed; however, when it occurs at inappropriate times (i.e., you are talking on the telephone) it is considered a mistaken goal.

As a single parent what can you do when the child's mistaken goal is attention? One thing you can do is give the child attention when something is being done correctly. If you give attention for appropriate behavior there will be less of a desire for the child to seek attention through misbehavior. You can also ignore minor misbehavior. However, if the child wants attention badly enough, some behaviors might occur that you should not ignore (i.e., the child is practicing biting on his baby sister). You should also remember that punishment is a form of attention. Children would rather be punished than ignored completely.

Power

Children whose mistaken goal is power usually feel that they belong only when they are in control or when they are proving others cannot boss them. The parent usually feels angry, provoked, or threatened and tends to fight or give in to the child. The child will usually continue the misbehavior when reprimanded. Why? Because the child feels important only when boss and to give in would be to admit the parent is the boss.

When you realize that you are involved in a power struggle the first thing to do is withdraw from the conflict. Many parents have a difficult time doing this because they feel to withdraw is to lose. However, by withdrawing the parent is really just saying "I know that we are not going to be able to work this out while we are both yelling and screaming at each other." At a better time the situation can be discussed in a calm manner.

Another thing to remember in working with power oriented children is to admit they have power and help them see how to use power in a constructive manner. Possibly the child could assume responsibility for a needed task and therefore become a boss. You should also realize that if you continue to fight with power oriented children you will only further convince them that it is important to have power.

Revenge

Children whose mistaken goal is revenge usually have given up on trying to belong by constructive means and decide to punish or get even with others. The parent usually feels deeply hurt and you wonder why the child can act this way after all you have done. Your typical reaction is to retaliate and get even. When you reprimand revengeful children they usually intensify their actions because they know they are being effective in getting back at you.

The parent working to correct the behavior of a revengeful child should avoid feeling hurt and avoid punishment and retaliation. You are asking yourself "after what the child did I'm going to wring his neck!" Now the behavior obviously cannot be allowed to continue when another person is being hurt; however, it is important not to punish or retaliate. If you do, the child is not likely to say "thanks I needed that," but rather feel that even you dislike and want to hurt him. You have to remember that the child's perception of what is happening is probably different than yours. You must try to build a trusting relationship and convince the child that she or he is loved. Remember you can love your child without having to approve of the behavior.

Inadequacy

Children whose mistaken goal is inadequacy feel that they are unable to accomplish tasks and meet the expectations of others. The parent usually feels despair and hopelessness. Your tendency is to finally agree with the child that nothing can be done. When you reprimand children who feel inadequate they usually respond passively or fail to respond to whatever is done. Usually no improvement is shown.

In helping a child who feels inadequate, the first thing you can do is to stop your criticism. This child has been made to feel that nothing is ever done that meets with your satisfaction. You should begin to recognize any positive attempt, no matter how small, the child makes to improve. You can also try to stress the strengths and assets in your child. Above all, do not get discouraged yourself.

Important Concepts

A feeling of competition between siblings discourages certain traits and stimulates the development of others.

The child's position in the family constellation influences but does not determine personality and behavior.

Family atmosphere is a major influence on the values and beliefs children in a family will acquire.

All behavior has a purpose. The goals of misbehavior are: attention, power, revenge, and inadequacy.

Your reactions and feelings about a child's misbehavior point to the purpose of that behavior.

The child's behavior can most effectively be influenced by changing your own behavior.

Show appreciation for the child's positive behaviors, unless they are meant only to gain attention.

Withdraw from power struggles.

Punishment stimulates further retaliation on the part of the revengeful child; therefore, express good will to improve the quality of the relationship.

A child who displays inadequacy is not unable; rather the child lacks belief in his or her ability.

Focus on the child's strength and assets.

3
Methods You Can Use to Correct Misbehavior

Every misbehaving child is discouraged and needs continuous encouragement. Dreikurs and Grey (1968) wrote that children need encouragement "just as a plant needs water and sunshine." It is difficult to acquire the art of encouragement because we tend to discourage ourselves and others; however, if we are to help our children we must become a source of encouragement.

Encouragement involves the ability to focus on the assets and strengths of your children to build their confidence and self-concept. According to Dinkmeyer and Dreikurs (1963) the parent who encourages (1) places value on the child as he is; (2) shows faith in the child and enables him to have faith in himself; (3) sincerely believes in the child's ability and wins his confidence while building his self-respect; (4) recognizes a job "well done;" gives recognition for effort; (5) utilizes the family group to facilitate and enhance the development of the child; (6) integrates the family group so that each child can be sure of his place in it; (7) assists in the development of the skills sequentially and psychologically based to permit success; (8) recognizes and focuses on strengths and assets; and (9) utilizes the interest of the child to energize constructive activity.

A feeling of encouragement can come from non-verbal gestures like a smile, wink, pat on the back, or similar behaviors. We can also show encouragement by what we say. Reiner (1967, pp. 72–73) offers the following phrases to be used to encourage your child:

1. "You do a good job of . . ." Children should be encouraged when they do not expect it, when they are not asking for it. It is possible to point out some useful act of contribution in each child. Even a comment about something small and insignificant to us, may have great importance to a child.
2. "You have improved in . . ." Growth and improvement is something we should expect from all children. They may not be where we would like them to be, but if there is progress, there is less chance for discouragement. Children will usually continue to try if they can see some improvement.
3. "We like (enjoy) you, but we don't like what you do." Children frequently feel disliked after having made a mistake or after misbehaving. A child should never think he or she is not liked. Rather, it is important to distinguish between the child and his or her behavior, between the act and the actor.
4. "You can help me (us, the others, etc.) by . . ." To feel useful and helpful is important to everyone. Children want to be helpful; we have only to give them the opportunity.
5. "Let's try it together." Children who think they have to do things perfectly are often afraid to attempt something new for fear of making a mistake or failing.

6. "So you made a mistake; now, what can you learn from your mistake." There is nothing that can be done about what has happened, but a person can always do something about the future. Mistakes can teach children a great deal, especially if they do not feel embarrassed for erring.

7. "You would like us to think you can't do it, but we think you can." This approach could be used when children say or convey the impression that something is too difficult for them and they hesitate to even try. An individual who tries and fails, has at least had the courage to try. Our expectations should be consistent with the child's ability and maturity.

8. "Keep trying. Don't give up." When a child is trying, but not meeting much success, a comment like this might be helpful.

9. "I'm sure you can straighten this out (solve this problem, etc.), but if you need any help, you know where you can find me." Adults need to express confidence that children are able and will resolve their own conflicts, if given a chance.

10. "I can understand how you feel (not sympathy, but empathy) but I'm sure you'll be able to handle it."

As a single parent you may do some things that serve to discourage your children, probably without even being aware. It is common for parents to compare siblings and foster competition. This serves to be discouraging for the child who is constantly doing poorer than the other siblings. After a while this child will either give up trying or resort to misbehavior. We should only compare children with themselves. Each child has particular strengths and abilities and it would be unfair to compare them with other children who have different assets.

Some times parents establish unreasonably high standards for their children. We must remember that to expect adult performances from children who lack the necessary abilities and maturity serves to discourage the children. Many times we also expect children to know how to do things without us ever having taken the time to teach them. We should make sure that the children have the skills to perform the task and that our standard for completion is a reasonable one.

Many parents spend time emphasizing the negative behaviors rather than the positive actions of their children. However, these parents usually are unaware that they are reinforcing the same negative behaviors they are trying to eliminate. A child would rather be punished than to be ignored. Parents must stress the positive behavior of their children because by doing so the children will increase the number of positive behaviors.

Frequently parents wait until a child has completely mastered a task before giving recognition. The unfortunate part about this is that many times the child gets discouraged before completely mastering the task. If the parent would give encouragement as the child showed improvement, then the likelihood of the child completing the task would be greatly improved.

Natural and Logical Consequences

Another effective method, besides encouragement, used to foster positive behavior in children is natural and logical consequences. Through natural consequences children experience the consequences of their own behavior without the intervention of the parent. The child who touches something hot will get burned. The child who refuses to eat will get hungry. Sometimes it might be too dangerous for the child to experience the natural consequences (i.e., child playing in the street might be struck by a car) and therefore we would utilize logical consequences. Logical consequences are arranged by the parent. For example if the child spills a glass of milk, it is the child's responsibility to clean it up.

The concept of using consequences in child rearing is certainly not new. Herbert Spencer (1885) advocated logical consequences almost one hundred years ago and cited this example:

> Having refused or neglected to pick up and put away things that children scattered about and thereby having entailed the trouble of doing this on someone else, the child should, on subsequent occasions, be denied the means of giving this trouble. When it next petitions for the toybox, the reply of its mamma should be, "The last time you had your toys you left them lying on the floor and Jane had to pick them up. Jane is too busy to pick up every day the things you leave around and I cannot do it myself, so if you will not put your toys away when you are done with them, I cannot let you have them (p. 170)."

Natural and logical consequences should be discussed with and understood by the child before they are applied. Consequences will only be effective when the parent applies them consistently. If parents only apply them once or twice, the child will soon take advantage of the inconsistency.

The concept of natural and logical consequences is not clear to many people. Some parents insist that it is the same as punishment. Dreikurs and Grey (1968) make the following distinctions between consequences and punishment:

Consequences	Punishment
1. Express the reality of the social order or the situation not of the person (Democratic).	Expresses the power of a personal authority (Authoritarian).
2. Logically related to the misbehavior.	Not logical, only an arbitrary connection between misbehavior and consequences.
3. Involves no element of moral judgement.	Inevitably involves some moral judgement.

4. Concerned only with what will happen now.	Deals with the past.
5. The relationship and atmosphere are friendly. Resentment is minimized.	Often anger is present either overtly or covertly. Resentment is frequent.
6. Develop intrinsic motivation and self discipline.	Depends on extrinsic motivation.
7. No submission or humiliation.	Often requires submission or humiliation.
8. Freedom of choice within limits.	No alternative or choice.
9. Consequences are acceptable.	Punishment is at best only tolerable.
10. Thoughtful and deliberate.	Often impulsive.
11. Child feels important.	Child feels belittled.
12. Choice given once only.	Often involves endless nagging.
13. Use action.	Uses talking and coercion.
14. The child accepts responsibility for his own actions.	The adult takes responsibility for the child's actions.
15. The adult is disengaged from negative involvement with the child.	Involvement is always negative.
16. Based on the concept of equality of worth between children and adults.	Based on superior-inferior relationship between children and adults—fear of punishment.
17. Implies that the child can work out his own problems.	Implies that only an adult is capable of solving the child's problems.

To illustrate how logical consequences might be used in a typical family situation, read the example below:

Mary usually played with her food and had to constantly be reminded to eat or she would seldom finish her meal. Mother became quite annoyed with Mary and thought that a six year old should not have to be constantly reminded.

How could Mary's mother apply logical consequences? Mother should talk to Mary at an appropriate time (other than when they are eating) and discuss the situation. Possibly Mary can think of a solution that both can agree on. If not, mother could tell Mary that they would have twenty minutes to eat and the dishes would be removed from the table whether or not everyone was finished. If a person was not finished, there would be no snacks until the next meal.

Many times just talking about the situation and the parent stating what will happen is enough to resolve the problem. However, if the parent has a history of saying one thing and doing another, you can bet the child will test the parent to see if there will actually be follow-through. In Mary's case let's assume that after twenty minutes she is still not finished. Mother would simply remove the dishes. If Mary complains about not being allowed to finish, mother could say something like "I'm sorry you didn't get a chance to finish; maybe at our next meal you will be able to eat a little faster." At that point mother should begin talking about another subject even though Mary might like to pursue the issue and get mother involved in an argument. When meal time comes again mother should not remind Mary, but simply again follow the consequences if necessary. If Mary finishes her meal on time, mother might want to say "You must be pleased that you were able to finish your meal." Note that mother is not saying how proud she is that Mary finished and what a good girl she is—this would not be encouragement.

Use of Choices

In applying the concept of logical consequences, it is important to offer the child a choice. This usually involves a choice between the appropriate behavior and a logical consequence.

Michael, age 4, enjoys playing with his toys but is considerably less enthusiastic about picking them up when he is finished. Father usually keeps reminding Michael and finally loses his temper and picks up the toys himself.

Father should first talk with Michael and ask for possible solutions. If no viable solution is presented, then father can explain what he is going to do. Father could tell Michael that he can play with the toys as long as he is responsible for picking them up. If father has to pick them up, he will put the toys away until Michael seems responsible enough to pick them up himself (like Spencer suggested in the previous section). The next time the toys are on the floor father could simply offer Michael the choice: "Would you like to pick up your toys or should I?" If Michael picks them up, use this opportunity to provide encouragement. If father picks them up, he should put them away for a reasonable amount of time. He should not tell Michael that he is a bad boy or anything like that. In a short period of time this consequence will usually be effective.

Important Concepts

A misbehaving child is a discouraged child.

Encouragement involves the ability to focus on the assets and strengths of your children.

Natural and logical consequences require children to be responsible for their own behavior.

Consequences should be used instead of punishment.

Whenever possible, give the child a choice between acceptable alternatives.

4
Improving Your Family Communications

It is sometimes difficult for the single parent, with the responsibility for raising children alone, to decide how to use authority and to determine when to involve the children in decision-making. A recently divorced parent, for example, may make all the decisions such as: where the family will live, job choices, and child care, only to be criticized by the children.

A way to facilitate a more harmonious family relationship involves the use of a democratic method of solving daily problems and planning activities called the family council. This is a structure which encourages the development of responsibility in children as well as allowing the peaceful resolution of situations which might otherwise cause much conflict among family members. The family as a group becomes the governing body making appropriate decisions which affect everyone in the group.

Thomas Poffenberger wrote a bulletin describing the family council and the information is reprinted here:[1]

> Are your children part of the family?
> What a *silly* question!
> And yet, do we always treat them as first-class family members?
> Do you assign your children chores and then tell them how to do the jobs?
> Do you sometimes fail to consult the youngsters when deciding where to go on a family outing?
> Do you run your children's parties for them?
> Do you buy things for your kids without having them in on the selection?
> Do you buy things for the home without a word to junior or sister?
> Do you ask Hobart to do little jobs on the spur of the moment when he is busy with his own interests?

What Parent Doesn't?

If we are honest with ourselves we would certainly answer "yes" to some of these questions, and we should. There are times when we, as parents, must make decisions without the help of our children. *But let's not leave Hobart out in the cold.* If we must answer "yes" to most of the above questions most of the time, it might be worthwhile to ask ourselves just what we mean when we refer to children as being *a part of the family.* It means more than just living at home. It should include giving them a voice in family affairs rather than giving them the feeling that they are left out in the making of family decisions.

---

1. Reprinted with permission of the Cooperative Extension Service, Oregon State University, Corvallis.

Teen-agers Comment

In a family relations class,[2] students were asked what features in family living had made their family life happy. One girl made the following remark:

> I think a very important detail that makes a family a united and happy one is the fact that each member of the family is respected and taken for his worth. In our family, each member is respected by the other members and we all have an equal voice in the forming of our family policies. We all try to be fair and look at both sides in all questions. This way each member feels a part, and no one feels dictated to or treated unfairly.

Children Resent Exploitation

Children need the feeling that we parents think of them as human beings with some rights along with the expectations that we have of them. Many of us ask our children to do chores that we ourselves don't like to do. If we don't like to do them, we can hardly expect our youngsters to show any great eagerness for such jobs. Of course, all parents are bound to do a little of this from time to time and it is not going to do any great harm. But, let's not overdo it.

Children Need Consideration

It pays off when we give consideration to the feelings of young people. If a mother had her friends over for a bridge game, how eager would she be to hear her husband call, "Stop your card game and come help me with the chores, dear!" Children feel the same way about being called away from their friends when they are engaged in some activity. This is particularly true of adolescents who appreciate being treated "grown-up" in front of their age-mates.

Responsibility

This is not to say that the children should not have responsibilities around the home. It is very important that they learn to do their part, but along with these responsibilities should go certain benefits. It is wise to let youngsters have some choice in the job or jobs that they should do and then allow them to do such tasks at their own convenience. Then they know ahead of time what they must do and so can plan their time accordingly. If a job is not done, a parent may need to step in occasionally to see that the youngster does it.

2. Taught by Lester A. Kirkendall, Associate Professor of Family Life at Oregon State University.

This approach helps the children to understand the importance of planning and finishing jobs.

Another student from the family life class remarked how important responsibilities around the home had been to him:

> A feature which has made for a happy home life is the realization that we all had a responsible part in the family unit. There were tasks that we all had to do—tasks which were not allotted to a certain person but which had to be worked out in the unit. It was a disciplined unit, and out of it came a pride in the accomplishments of the family because we all knew that each had had some small part in them. Along with this came a sense of the family's interest in me and trust that I could be depended upon. I knew that whatever the case was they would be interested and would trust my decisions.

A Voice in Decisions

Let's take a problem. Most parents of teen-agers go 'round and 'round over the question of how late they may stay out. When a certain time limit is suggested to them, no matter how fair it may be, they seem to resent it. A better angle is to ask them what time they feel they should be home. When this approach is used, parents are often surprised to find that kids are "harder" on themselves then they, the parents, would have been. Anyone would be rash to guarantee this, but then, parents have the last word in case the request is to return at 3 A.M.

Children want rules, but they want a voice in making them.

Youngsters want to have rules for regulation of some sort seems to give them a feeling that their parents love them as well as a sense of security. In a recent study,[3] one teen-ager remarked that she guessed her parents didn't care anything about her because she could stay out as late as she wanted while all the rest of the girls had to be in at a certain time. Even though teen-agers often rebel at parental concern this remark illustrates their need to feel that their parents have a vital interest in their welfare.

In regard to the feeling of security that rules give youngsters, one authority likened it to driving a car across the Golden Gate bridge. Most of us feel pretty safe in driving across the bridge, but if there were no guard rails, we would feel mighty uncomfortable! Yet time after time we drive across without ever using the rails to stay on the bridge—it just gives us a very comfortable feeling to know they are there! Youngsters feel much the same way about rules. Even if they don't bump into them, they like to know they are there and they like to have a voice in making the rules in the first place.

---

3. "Attitudes of Some Adolescent Girls Toward Their Parents" HE 4–475 (a study of 252 4-H girls) by Thomas Poffenberger, Oregon State University Extension Service.

Easier on Parents

Let's take another example. Teen-agers want many things that are out of the financial reach of the family. However, because of their social need to be accepted by their age-mates, it is important to them to have the same things that their friends have—regardless of cost. When Mary Jane comes in and requests the latest clothes fad, she can't understand why she can't have it just because mother says, "There isn't enough money to buy it." She sees money going out for all kinds of things and thinks there must be enough for something that is so important to her. However, if the girl has a chance to sit around the family table and discuss finances, she will get a different picture. Father states the amount of money available for the month. So much must go for rent, so much to pay off the family car, so much for food, etc., and there are a few dollars left over. How shall they be spent? Hobart needs a new pair of shoes, and Mary Jane needs the latest fad. If this approach is used, her parents may well hear her say, "Brother needs the new shoes more than I need anything right now." She understands why she cannot have it this month and then can be casual about her altruism to her friends. At the same time, she is learning the many different places where money must go in running a household.

In Business, Too

More and more industries are becoming aware of the importance of consulting employees on matters which concern them. They are also recognizing the benefits to be gained by making employees feel that they are a part of the company. Workers who receive stock or other interests in a corporation feel that the business is theirs as well as the management's. The results in increased productivity are great! This principle is certainly worth applying in our own families. By considering our children as individuals who can help and letting them have a voice in family affairs, we will be making family life more enjoyable for all, and we will be doing a better job of preparing our youngsters for their own family life later on.

Training in Family Finance

Many young married couples have quite a shock when they are first confronted with money problems. They seem to have no idea what it costs to run a household and raise a family. As a result, they often get themselves into a lot of financial hot water in the early years of marriage. Such young people can hardly be expected to know much about family finance since they had little or no opportunity to learn about handling money as they were growing up in their own families.

Those who have had a "say" in family finances, such as the college student quoted below, will be in a better position to make sound decisions in the future.

> Financial difficulties were discussed with us when we were old enough to realize their importance. Just last Thanksgiving vacation, my father asked me if I thought he should sell our store. He then presented the facts and figures of the business and the price offered him. After a couple of days of thought I gave him my opinion.

The best way to teach youngsters about finances is to let them take part in the actual handling of family business. Some fathers don't "warm" to such an idea. A usual comment is, "If I told Hobart how much I made, it would be all over town in half an hour!" However, this is not likely to occur if Papa makes no great to-do about the amount of his income. In fact, if the youngster is made to feel that he is a real part of the family, he can be counted on to guard any family secret.

Some fathers also think they would lose respect if their income were known because the family believes it is greater than it really is. If that is the way father wants it he is asking for trouble! The family is bound to make more requests for money than "Pop" can fill. And, if he thinks he is getting respect by putting up a false front, he is pretty wrong!

Parental Understanding

Many research studies have clearly demonstrated that children do not evaluate their parent's worth in terms of how much money they have, but rather in terms of their understanding and closeness to them.

In the author's study previously mentioned, over 50 per cent of the 252 girls reported that the one thing they needed most from their parents was, "guidance, understanding, and help with problems." Some of the comments individuals made regarding their needs were:

> Being able to talk to them (parents) without being embarassed. Guidance through life so that when the time comes I'll be able to face decisions with confidence.
>
> Understanding and listening to your problems even if they aren't important to them.
>
> Consideration and to let me make my own decisions and have certain responsibilities at home instead of just being expected to do the right thing at the right time.

The Purdue Public Opinion Panel questioned thousands of school youths regarding their feelings on various problems. Only one per cent checked the statement, "I'm ashamed of my father's job," while the statement receiving the largest percentage of checks (21%) was, "I can't discuss personal things with my parents."

A Family Council

If we want to give a name to a family discussion group, we might call it a Family Council. This may sound a bit formal, but it need not be so at all. In fact, some of the most productive discussions can take place during a meal. The important thing is that such get-togethers occur whenever anything comes up that affects family members. It should include such topics as where to go on vacation or plans for a family picnic as well as family finances.

A family council should include every member of the family who is old enough to express an opinion on the subject being discussed. Three-year-old Hobart may well have an opinion on whether to go to the zoo or to the park on the family outing but could throw little light on whether or not the family homestead should be sold. Therefore, it would be logical to include him in the first discussion but rather illogical to include him in the second.

The Family Council at Work

Here are some more comments made by teen-age college students looking back on their family life. They seem to be pretty well sold on the idea of the family council.

Another thing that tended to bring our family close together was the fact that we did things together. Even now that I am older, I still have the desire to do things with my parents. When we go on a trip, we go together. Also when we work, we work together. This has tended to develop from a pleasant attitude toward each other in all things we do and say. Even though one of us may want to go somewhere else, we have a very effective way of choosing where to go. We all put down on a slip of paper where we want to go and what we want to do. Then the youngest one puts all the slips in a hat and then draws one out. Whatever it says is what we do on our vacation or trip. In this way by the law of averages, in the end we all get to do something each one wants to do.

Another thing that made my family life happy was the ability of all persons to discuss what each had done that day. This gave the other members of the family a chance to assist and advise. This was particularly good in my case as I was the youngest and thereby the least experienced. This discussion was usually carried on in the evening at the dinner table. One big advantage to this discussion was that, even though the person discussing his problem could not work out a solution, he had the feeling that he was not shouldering it alone. As far back as I can remember, no important decisions were made in the family without each member hearing about it and offering his or her opinions. One example of this is when we sold our place, we all got to put our own opinions in on what we would keep and what we would bring with us. On our trip out here, whenever we decided to do something such as visiting relatives or even going to a show, the decision was made by all of us and not one. One of the reasons this worked is we had all learned to "give in" part of the time. If things were done the way I wanted one time, I knew that I should be willing to do what someone else wanted the next time.

When a family problem arises, we discuss it together, working it out for satisfactory results for each member of the family. In this way no one can hold a grudge for something which happened within our family.

Freedom of Expression

The most important aspect of a family council is frankness. Children need the feeling that they can speak their own minds, otherwise the council does not serve its purpose. Parents need to encourage such frankness by being frank themselves and by trying to understand their youngsters' point even if they take a dim view of the idea. Of course, when children are young, it is necessary for parents to take most of the responsibility for decisions, but as kids grow older, it is important that parents begin to withdraw and give them more and more voice in the decisions to be made. Remember, that in a short time they will have to be making lots of decisions—and most of them without help from parents! There is no better way to prepare them to handle problems as adults than to give them ever increasing experience in handling problems as they are growing older.

A Guiding Hand

This does not mean that children should be allowed to over-rule the parents in every decision and get anything they want. Often their level of experience will lead to poor conclusions and parents must use veto powers. But it is sometimes surprising how clearly youngsters can reason when given the chance! Occasionally, when kids make plans that parents do not think are too wise, if it is not too important an issue, it may be well to let them have their way. If their plans are really unsound, they will find out their mistake soon enough, and that is a most effective way to learn. If children can learn by making mistakes on small matters they will be better prepared to make sound decisions later on.

Points for Parents

Giving our children a real part in the family "pays off" in many ways.

It gives them the feeling that "this is my family" and makes them more willing to take responsibility in it.

It reduces general complaining since they feel they have been consulted about an issue.

It gives them the feeling that their parents are considering them as individuals rather than something to be exploited.

It gives them valuable experience in learning to make decisions, in taking responsibility, and in learning to handle family finances.

It gives them experience in the democratic way of life.

If you decide to begin a family council, the idea should be discussed informally and a time established for the first meeting when all family members can attend. It is important that meetings be held on a planned basis, usually once a week. When a time for the first meeting has been established, all family members should be invited to participate. The children may have several questions and be sure to tell them that attendance is not compulsory, however, decisions will be made regardless of the number of family members who attend. A request for agenda items can be posted at some easily accessible spot like the refrigerator door. Children too young to write can have an older sibling or yourself write their concern on the agenda.

At the first meeting the single parent should explain that in order for the council to function, some ground rules should be established that are acceptable to all. A typical rule might be that only one person talk at a time. Family members might suggest other rules.

One of the most important rules relates to the concept of concensus rather than majority rule. It is not possible for the children, who frequently outnumber the parent in votes to enact an increase in allowance, for example, unless the parent agrees to that increase. Everyone, including the parent must agree before any policy is set or any rules changed. This concept reinforces the idea of equality, each member of the family has an equal say in the running of the family.

The single parent should act as the presiding officer at the initial meeting so that younger children get an idea of how to conduct a meeting. The parent should ask if someone would be willing to take minutes and later post them at a designated place. If there are no volunteers (and there may not be because the children are probably still unsure of what is happening), the parent should take notes. The group should then decide on a system of selecting a chairperson and secretary for each meeting (preferably on a rotating basis so each member has an opportunity to perform each function).

Discussion of agenda items usually follows this sequence:

1. The person who put the first item on the agenda is asked to explain the concern.
2. Everyone has an opportunity to express their opinion.

3. Alternative ideas and/or solutions are presented.
4. Consensus on one of the ideas is achieved (or postponed to the next meeting).
5. The person who placed the next item on the agenda would explain the concern (if all items have been covered, the chairperson can either ask for additional items or move for adjournment).

After the initial meeting a regular order of business can be followed utilizing this outline:

1. Minutes of the last meeting are read.
2. Discuss some activity the family can do for fun (i.e., going out for pizza, visiting the zoo, going to the park).
3. Planning the coming week.
4. Discuss the agenda items.
5. Ask for any additional agenda items.
6. Adjourn until the next meeting.

If no one other than the single parent chooses to come to the first meeting, the parent should hold the meeting alone. Catlin (1976) described how one mother handles this situation. Jane was the mother of three children aged 8, 11, and 13 and presented the idea of a family council one Sunday morning. The children refused to participate so Jane sat down at the table and proceeded with the meeting by herself. She explained to the empty chairs that she felt there were many family matters that the children could help with and that she had not considered their opinions seriously enough in the past. She then came to a decision about the time that the council would meet each week, served herself the snack that was prepared for after the meeting, and posted the minutes of the meeting on the kitchen bulletin board without comment to anyone.

The next week she again sat by herself at the table at the appointed hour and this time she brought up a problem she had regarding the messy kitchen that usually existed after the three children had finished afternoon snacks. She decided that she was not willing to cook supper in such a messy place and that if it got as late as 6:00 P.M. and the kitchen still was not clean, she would go out to eat. She again had the snack and posted the minutes on the bulletin board.

Although the children complained about the rule, mother said nothing. For the next three nights the kitchen was a mess so mother went out for supper. She cooked in the kitchen for two successive days and the next day again went out to eat.

The following day was the regular meeting time for the family council and this time the oldest girl came. They planned a family activity and made decisions regarding the use of the family car. The daughter raised the issue of an increase in her allowance so she could learn more about effective budgeting and mother agreed. The two enjoyed the snack and the minutes were posted as usual.

As could be expected, everyone was present at the next meeting and participated in the decision-making process. If the mother had threatened, coerced or manipulated the children to attend the council meetings, she would have failed to involve the whole family positively in democratic problem solving. Jane should be congratulated because she did not get discouraged when the children initially chose not to be involved. Mother's patience and maintaining a pleasant, friendly attitude, enabled her to avoid a power struggle over attendance at the meetings. The only negative aspect of the situation was that mother did not allow sufficient notice in advance before the first meeting was held.

Some readers may feel that Jane's action of going out to eat may seem cruel, however, it was her way of applying logical consequences. Other single parents might have used different consequences especially if the children were too young to leave alone. The important point, however, is that the council was used as a means of resolving a family problem and offers promise for the future.

If a family council is to be effective, it must meet the following criteria outlined by Dreikurs, Gould, and Corsini (1974):

1. Equality of all members.
2. Mutual respect.
3. Open communication.
4. Regularity.
5. Agenda rules.
6. Joint deliberation.
7. Reciprocal responsibility.
8. Mutual decision.

It would be impossible for a group of individuals living together as a family to get along perfectly at all times. The family council serves as a mechanism for resolving problems as smoothly as possible. Single parents can help make the council work by supporting council decisions, refusing to make decisions that should be first discussed at the council, discussing all agenda items even if they seem unimportant and participating as an equal member of the family.

Single parents can gain more cooperation from their children by establishing family meetings. In the single-parent home, family meetings are restricted to the discussion of matters other than the children's relationship with the absent parent. This topic should be discussed at another time. Family meetings are for the purpose of making decisions about issues that involve those living together.

In closing, please strongly consider the possibility of initiating a council in your family. One of the major problems with families today is a lack of communication. The council will serve as a vehicle for all members of the family to discuss their concerns. And please, do not just try the council once. Give the idea a fair chance even if you have to use your ingenuity like Jane did to get it started. You will never regret your efforts.

Important Concepts

The Family Council is a regularly scheduled meeting of all family members to discuss common concerns and to plan family activities.

Take time to give recognition for the accomplishments and improvement of family members.

All family members participate as equals.

Rotate serving as chairperson and secretary.

Focus on what the family can do rather than on what individual members should do.

Try to understand each other's point of view.

Follow through on all decisions made at the council meeting. Poor decisions can be discussed at the next meeting.

The Family Council is designed to aid in making decisions about issues that involve family members living together, therefore, the absent parent in single parent families should not be discussed at the council meeting.

5
Summarizing
Child Rearing Techniques

In this book we have discussed several child rearing principles. Encouragement has been described as the foundation upon which other techniques should be built. Examples of how consequences and choices could help in resolving child rearing problems were presented. The Family Council was suggested as a method to improve family communications. Before we begin the section of the book pertaining to resolving specific problems, it seems appropriate to summarize some fundamental child rearing techniques. Ken Marlin[1] described thirty-four suggestions for parents, listed words and actions that encourage, and dispelled five myths that sabotage parents. This material is reprinted here as a summary of child rearing techniques.

The Basics of Practical Parenting

1. The Golden Rule of Parenting:
Without doubt the BASIC basic of practical parenting is the *golden rule.* When parents really do unto their children as they would have children do unto them, children try their best to satisfy. The parent who trusts his children usually gets trust back. Parents who are courteous with children usually get courtesy in return. Most parents who have trouble with their children do not realize the many ways that they themselves actually demonstrate or model the very behavior they object to in their children.

2. The Marvel of Mutual Respect:
Mutual respect is the cement that bonds personal relationships together. Parents repeatedly complain that they get no respect from their children. Ordinarily it takes only a little observation of such parents and their children together to see where the child learned to be disrespectful. *Too often parents act superior to their children,* as though they are masters and the children slaves.

They belittle their children, insult them, treat them as inferiors—then expect the children to respect them!

Parents who respect their children treat them as equally important persons. They listen to their children talk about their ideas and opinions. They don't make fun of them. By respecting their children, they enable them to learn to respect themselves. Children who have self-respect find it easier to respect others, including parents!

3. Two Basic Laws of Human Action:
Not too many parents recognize that human behavior is closely related to *two ironclad laws of the universe:* (1) a body in motion tends to remain in motion: and (2) a body at rest tends to stay at rest.

---

1. Reprinted by permission of Practical Parenting Publications, Columbia, MO., and Ken Marlin.

In much the same way, the child whose body is in motion (such as playing a game when it's bedtime) will probably try to continue what he's doing. The child whose body is not doing something (such as cleaning his room or not carrying out the trash) will usually stoutly resist demands that he stop sitting in front of the TV and go into motion.

Practical parents avoid raw displays of force or power. They realize that using pressure to start or stop actions of their child fails more often than it succeeds. Instead, they look for approaches that motivate and *help the child want to cooperate.* They work at establishing a good relationship with their child. When parent-child relations are warm and harmonious, *children are far more willing to* comply with the desires of their parents—without need for constant parent pulling or pushing.

4. Even Infants Are Basically Different:

People *are* different—literally from birth. Brand new infants show marked variety in activity level, acceptance of changes in routine, sensitivity to pain, general mood level, persistence and attention span, to name only a few.

Does this mean that parents must treat each child individually? The answer is yes—and no.

Definitely, a parent should respect his child, including the child's inborn differences. *A parent needs to resist using pressure* to remold the child in the parent's image.

Still, some children display such extreme differences that they obviously need help in learning to control impulses that are in conflict with the rights and differences of others, including parents!

Parents who respect both the child and themselves try to overlook or tolerate differences that really don't matter anyway—as most don't. But they try to help the child modify differences that will prove a handicap later on when he reaches adulthood.

The practical parenting approach suggested in this booklet provides many guidelines to help the parent help his child learn to handle his innate differences constructively instead of destructively, and without resorting to constant parent coercion. Force nearly always backfires by widening differences and making them even more pronounced.

5. All Behavior Has a Purpose:

Few parents seem to realize that each and all child behavior has meaning and purpose. To understand what makes a child tick, it is necessary for parents to understand what the child's goal is when he misbehaves.

Five major goals were identified by Dr. Rudolf Dreikurs. They are: (1) to belong to and cooperate within one's family, community and society. (2) To keep others busy by demanding constant attention and services. (3) To win out over others—to defy, boss or best them. (4) To get even with or hurt others who we believe have hurt us. (5) To be excused from functioning, to withdraw, appear helpless, not cooperate with the expectations of others.

According to Dr. Dreikurs, a child's misbehavior results from discouragement and mistaken ideas about how to find a place in the family. The parent who fails to grasp the true meaning of misbehavior is likely to respond to the child in ways that do not bring about better behavior.

How can a parent recognize the purpose of his child's behavior and then cope with it most appropriately? Interestingly enough, the parent can do this by becoming aware of his own emotional reaction. Through checking his own feelings and using the following system, the parent can unmask the child's goal—quickly and easily.

But merely recognizing the goal isn't quite enough. Different child goals call for different parent responses. Following are brief descriptions of child behavior that typically goes with each goal, kinds of parent feelings that enable a parent to spot the child's goal, and effective parent responses to each goal that help the child.

Goal of Child with Healthy Sense of Self-worth

To Belong and Cooperate
The child fits in, is interested in and contributes to family events and welfare; puts out active efforts to cooperate with others; is willing to negotiate and compromise differences. It's easy to recognize this child's goal; the parent feels good and satisfied with child.

Goals of Discouraged Children

To Gain (Demand) Attention
This child may act cute or make a nuisance of himself. "Pesters" the parent. If parent feels sharp annoyance, or impatience, it is likely child's goal is to win attention. Unwise parent response: Scold child for bothering—or give in when child demands attention. Either response fulfills child's purpose. More effective response: Ignore child's demands for attention as he is making them, but resolve to give child more positive attention when he is not exerting pressure. Remember this: the attention-seeking child has been taught to be that way! Parents have failed to give this child enough notice at those times when he has sought to belong, contribute and cooperate. Parents often reap what they earlier sowed when they were too busy to bother with the child when he needed attention.

To Gain Power
The child who seeks to win out over a parent is sassy, stubborn, contradictory, unruly, disobedient, lazy, continually forgetting, and-or rebellious. When parent feels anger, rage ("he can't get away with this—I'll show him who's boss in this family!") it's a sure bet that the child's goal is to show his

power and win out over the parent. Unwise parent response: Fight the child. Punish him for his disrespect. Criticize, scold and lecture the child. More effective parent response: Recognize and frankly admit to the child that you have been wrong to try to command and force him, that you can't make him do what you wish (which is the truth, by the way), that you wish to work out a better solution. Then negotiate.

To Gain Revenge

The child who seeks revenge finds ways to disappoint and hurt parents. This child has decided he can't win by slugging it out with the parent, so he resorts to more subtle, underhanded methods for showing his power to get even. A girl with this goal may humiliate her parents by getting pregnant. Both boys and girls may steal and get caught. A lot of drug experimentation and addiction may have the hidden purpose of getting even with the parents. Parent can recognize this goal by their feelings of outrage and deep resentment. Unwise parent response: Punish the child. Hurt him in return for his hurt. Apply even more restrictions and penalties for misbehavior than before. More effective parent response: Admit you've been unwise in trying to dominate the child. Recognize you have mistakenly sought to win out rather than work problems out with the child. Forgive the child and try to show him you value him. Do not satisfy child's purpose by being disappointed. Use child's behavior as a signal that he needs help and your efforts have been misdirected. You've failed to recognize you're dealing with a very discouraged child.

To Withdraw

This child may pretend to be stupid, may make silly mistakes when you give him a task, may spend a lot of time alone in his room. He tries to demonstrate he is incapable of being relied upon. A parent can recognize this goal by his own feeling of hopelessness, by his confusion about what to do, by the urge to throw up his hands in defeat. This child has reached the conviction that he can't win at anything, that being passive is the only way to make it. Unwise parent response: Give up on the child. Try to force him to come out of his shell. Tell him how inadequate he is, how disappointed you are. More effective parent response: Find occasions to show appreciation for the child. Tell him you want to help, that you won't give up on him. Avoid giving notice to child's complaints and failures. Do acknowledge any positive, useful, and helpful behavior the child displays. Don't respond to the child's discouragement by getting discouraged yourself.

The last two purposes, and especially when the child seeks to withdraw a lot, often call for professional help. They show such an extreme degree of family conflict and child discouragement that the parent may not be able to improve the situation without the aid of some experienced person outside the family.

6. Pitfalls of Punishment, Rewards and Praise:

Many parents bank heavily on punishment, rewards and praise for controlling their children. This reliance is understandable since such methods have been long and widely used as social management methods. They date back beyond the days of lords and serfs, in fact.

But few parents, living in our modern democratic era, ever really stop to ask themselves how they react when someone in power punishes, rewards or flatters them. Do they really feel better—or do they feel manipulated or put down and resentful?

Following are some seldom considered consequences of these often overused policies of child training and discipline:

PUNISHMENT

May teach children that might makes right, that only force counts.
Can sabotage parent efforts to build genuine mutual respect.
Frequently invites children to retaliate or get even.
Is used by many children to justify future misbehavior.
Often is deliberately sought by children seeking attention.
Shows parent bankruptcy—that the parent does not know how to use positive disciplinary approaches and methods.

REWARDS

Can easily become bribery for behavior parent wants.
May teach child to behave only when some token is offered.
Often buy bad behavior when rewards are withheld.
Frequently cause dickering between parent and child over how much reward is enough, causing anxiety for everyone.
Contribute to one-up, one-down relationship between parent and child instead of a sense of cooperative equality in the family.
Discourage child from behavior out of sense of personal responsibility.

PRAISE (Flattery)

Often is an easily-recognized control gimmick that is resented.
May be disrespectful of child's own judgment of his actions.
Can convince child his value depends on performance, not him.
Frequently is embarrassing when child is disappointed with self.
Can cause child to distrust parent judgment and intelligence.

How much better it is for everyone concerned when parents focus more on seeking to improve basic relationships with their children—and rely less on bribery and physical coercion. Certainly, there are some cases where a professional family counselor may develop a treatment plan that utilizes rewards, punishment and/or praise to help the child. But in normal family living less use of these methods seems to bring richer family relationships and easier cooperation between family members.

7. *Amazing Power of Consequences:*

Practical Parents have learned to use everyday situations, instead of personal force, to teach their children. They rely on the results to the child of these events to do the trick. There are two kinds of results or consequences— natural consequences and logical consequences—that are powerful training aids. Consequences allow the child to learn what happens when he does or doesn't do certain things. For instance, the child who leans back on a chair and falls (a natural consequence of leaning back too far) learns not to do it again, because it hurts. No parent lecture is necessary to get this across. The child learns to be more careful without advice from anyone. Logical consequences are deliberately chosen by the parent to help the child learn to follow family and social requirements.

Example of using logical results or consequences: A child repeatedly comes home late for supper, disrupting family mealtime. Mother and father don't scold. Instead, they calmly but firmly notify the child that, in the future, no food will be served to members who arrive late for dinner. It will be assumed when this happens that the tardy person is not hungry and the setting will be removed.

Next time the child is not on time for a meal parents do exactly as they promised—remove his plate. Then when the child comes home, even if he pleads, cries or throws a tantrum, parents stand firm and decline to permit the child to eat until next mealtime. This approach has been highly successful, when parents have the heart to follow it consistently. The child quickly learns to be home on time for meals when it's in his interest to do so.

Natural and logical consequences permit the child to learn what happens when he behaves in certain ways. But—the parent must be very careful in using logical consequences not to boss or punish the child or it will backfire.

Natural and logical consequences teach the child to behave well and responsibly for the positive benefits he receives in return—either avoiding pain or gaining benefits he desires.

The genuinely helpful parent allows the child to learn through results of his behavior and avoids using personal authority through constant reminders and punishment.

Only in moments of real danger is it necessary for parents to protect the child from his actions. A skinned knee—even a broken bone—is far better than a babied child. Logical results are highly workable when parents resist impulses to make them a form of punishment. Natural consequences always work to improve the child's behavior when parents are able to refrain from interference. But when parents can't resist the impulse to moralize, they destroy the usefulness of both kinds of consequences.

8. Encouragement Makes Kids Glow:

Children need encouragement just as much as flowers and trees need sunshine and water to thrive. Encouraging parents emphasize what's right about their children instead of always telling them what's wrong. Their communications to children are filled with "You cans" instead of "You can'ts." These parents seldom overlook a chance to let their children know they are accepted, appreciated and respected just as they are instead of as they could or should be. Through having and showing such faith in their children, encouraging parents help their children to have more faith in themselves.

All of us realize we really don't do anything well when our own morale is low, when we are discouraged. There is considerable evidence that children misbehave only when they are unhappy in their family relations and discouraged about their ability to succeed by useful means.

9. The Attention That Gets Positive Results:

Being interested in and friendly toward the child is the kind of parent attention that counts. Constantly criticizing, yelling at, showing disappointment with and punishing separate parent and child from one another. Children who begin to believe they can't get positive parent attention often misbehave just to get their parents to notice and become involved with them. They become convinced that unpleasant attention is better than none at all. So, in many instances when parents bawl their children out, crab at them, and scold, they give the child exactly what he wants! So he continues the behavior that prompted the criticism.

10. Pause Before Pouncing:

When the child misbehaves—think before acting. This, however, is just the opposite of what hosts of parents do in a tense situation. By acting on their first impulse, these parents may be giving the child the very attention he is seeking. Or, if in the middle of a power struggle, they may intensify it.

There are four steps the overly-impulsive parents needs to learn to take: (1) Deliberately stop, look and listen to what's happening. (2) Decide what the unwise thing to do would be and don't do it. (3) Recognize what the child expects you to do—and do the opposite. (4) Communicate when your anger has abated. This procedure breaks up the game and makes possible a more constructive solution through calm negotiation.

11. Invest in Training Time:

Practical Parents take time for training the child in skills and habits necessary for satisfying living. Many parents overlook the need to set aside specific times for teaching, especially when the child is very young. It should be undertaken only during quiet, friendly periods. Trying to train the child when you are upset or when other people are around is usually doomed to fail. It takes time to teach children how to behave, but when parents don't take the time they invariably end up taking much more time correcting the untrained child.

12. Minimize Mistakes:

Literally millions of parents have a very bad habit that sharply reduces any chance for peaceful and pleasant influence over their children. They overreact to the everyday mistakes their children make. They just don't realize and accept the fact that everyone makes blunders, and lots of them—even parents. Nobody's perfect. But to dwell on mistakes and feel a lot of guilt or indignation over them only serves to make matters worse. Treating mistakes as learning experiences usually is a much more productive way to handle them.

When parents focus a lot of attention on their child's mistakes, one of several things happens—and none of them is good for either child or parent. If the child's goal is to get attention, the parent's annoyance gives the child exactly what he seeks. If the child's goal is power, the mistake and his parent's angry response to it can be a perfect springboard into a loud family brawl. And finally, for the child who already feels worthless, his mistakes, accompanied by constant parent criticism, can serve as an ideal excuse for his further withdrawal and defeat.

Parents in counseling who learn to ignore most child mistakes (including a lot of what is typically called misbehavior), and who master the art of paying more attention to positive child behavior, usually end up having more success and happier times with their children. Practical Parents allow their children to learn from the consequences of their errors—at every possible opportunity.

13. Vanishing as Effective Parent Action:

In moments of conflict with children—vanish! Leave the room. Retire to the bathroom. Never give attention to the child who is demanding it with belligerent, disrespectful behavior. There is no satisfaction to the child in throwing a temper tantrum when he loses his audience or fellow combatant. Walking away from the power struggle gives tempers a chance to cool and lets the parent's brain reactivate to examine what's happening and find a more sensible solution than fighting. Beware buying the idea you have to do something in every situation. Doing nothing can be an affective tactic in handling conflict. Children need plenty of positive attention when they behave, but no negative attention when they misbehave.

14. Do Only What You Can Do:

When a lot of things go wrong, parents frequently try to tackle everything all at once. By attempting this impossible task, they set themselves up to fail.

They demand and command and threaten the child with dire results if he doesn't behave as the parent wishes. But often such warnings are without meaning because the parent can't make them stick. Practical Parents limit their discipline efforts to areas where they can enforce rules merely by being consistently firm.

15. Action—Much Better Than Words:

Lecturing, moralizing, scolding, criticizing (talking, talking, talking!) are the most commonly found verbal sounds found in families where there's lots of friction between parents and children. Children in these families become "parent deaf." Finally, they listen only when they become convinced punishment is forthcoming. Usually the child knows very well what's expected of him. Practical Parents never tell a child something he already knows or something he's been told before. They never talk to punish. They talk to be friendly, to work out rather than win out.

Suppose the parent is driving down the road and the children start acting up or fighting. Avoid the impulse to yell at them and demand they knock it off. Instead, simply stop the car at the side of the road and calmly wait for the children to agree to be quiet if you agree to drive on. Many parents report this to be a magic tactic.

16. Overdemanding Parents:

Parents often ask too much of their children. Practical Parents learn the difference between demanding more than the child can do and expecting him to do what he can do. For example, if a child has learned to tie his shoes, he should be expected always to tie them. But he shouldn't be required to be the best shoe tier in town. Too many parents pressure their children to be at the top in school grades, sports or in social skills. They browbeat their children to try harder and do better. Children can easily conclude they are failures if they don't live up to their parent's expectations. Often they become discouraged and unwilling even to try to do what they are capable of doing.

17. Overprotecting Parents:

Without realizing it, the parent who gives unnecessary service to a child who can do things for himself is teaching that child to feel helpless, useless, and inferior. These unneeded efforts tell the child: "You are too small, too inadequate, too poor in judgment, just not good enough." Such parents, who sincerely believe they are giving are actually taking from the child—taking away his self-respect and sense of achievement.

By unintentionally discouraging the child, the overprotective parent also may teach the child not to be responsible for himself, to grow up dependent rather than independent and self-reliant. For example, a child who chronically forgets everything invariably is found to have a parent who never forgets anything—especially does he never forget to remind the child! Parents, in spite of the temptation to help, must resist giving in to it, must learn to mind their own business. Instead, on all possible occasions, they need to allow a child to experience the consequences of what he does or fails to do.

18. Sympathy Can Be Destructive:

When parents bestow too much attention on a hurt or sick child, they help him learn to feel sorry for himself. The child who learns self-pity can all too easily become emotionally fragile for life. Children usually are far less harmed by an injury or personal tragedy than they are by the over-concern of well-meaning parents, relatives or friends. Being physically crippled seems to be much less damaging to the child than having parents who feel pity for him. Satisfaction in life depends on our learning to take whatever comes in stride.

19. Unhealthy Dependence:

Some parents are convinced they must constantly remind their children what to do and do things for them that they should learn to manage for themselves. When this happens, children are deprived of opportunities to take responsibility for themselves. At the same time, these parents learn to depend on their ability to help children for their own feelings of importance. Then, when they can no longer keep themselves busy with their children, these parents find themselves feeling useless and forlorn. Needless to say, Practical Parents avoid falling into the trap of such unwholesome dependence.

20. Coping with Children's Fears:

Children often learn that being afraid, requiring constant attention and reassurance, is a fine way to monopolize the parent's time and tyrannize the family. A certain amount of fear is common among children. But it can become a serious problem when parents respond to a child's fright with sympathy or pity. Doing this actually trains the child to be fearful by rewarding the emotion.

Practical Parents minimize displays of fright. They check what is happening to be sure there is no real danger, calmly assure the child that he'll be able to handle the situation, then in a kindly but firm way expect the child to do what he is using fear to avoid doing. Such parents realize when they make a big deal of fear they make fear a big deal with the child.

21. Handling the Bossy or Sassy Child:

Here's a sobering fact. The child who tries to be boss usually has a parent who seeks to boss. The child who sasses his parent most often has a sassy parent. Parents who seek to have their own way all the time actually model the same kind of expectation and behavior to their children. Unfortunately, being blind to their own behavior, parents often don't easily recognize this. The Practical Parent asks or otherwise induces the child to do what is needed and avoids bossy pressure—and usually, with a little patience, gets the behavior wanted from the child.

22. When Children Lie:

The parent who is morally outraged when he catches his child in a lie is not helping the child learn to do better. Like all human behavior, lying invariably serves a purpose. Children lie to avoid punishment, to make themselves feel important, or to defy parents. By their harsh response, by condemning and punishing the child, parents unwittingly promote lying instead of reducing it. Parents need to analyze carefully their relationship with the child to find out what's gone wrong, then correct it. Preaching at, scolding, or yelling at a child for lying may backfire completely by convincing him he is a bad person. And this only serves to discourage the child further.

23. When Children Fight:

Many—probably most—fights between or among children are deliberately provoked to get parent attention. When children learn that fighting keeps parents busy with them, they are likely to continue having conflicts. By separating them and/or acting as judge, parents fall into the trap of rewarding children's dramatics and stimulating them to fight even more.

An important fact to remember: Fights require cooperation! When children fight they are actually working together. A child can't fight by himself. If one fighter doesn't want to continue, the fight stops. Parents should never try to find out who started the fight. Nor should they punish one child and feel sorry for the other. When two children fight, both are to blame because each is willing to participate. When parents stay out of fights children usually begin getting along lots better. One coping method parents have found very effective is to permit fighting, but insists on the rule that all fights take place out of doors.

24. Dealing with Pressure from Outsiders:

Parenthood is loaded with well-meaning advice of outsiders about how children should be reared. Most parents yearn for approval from other adults—especially approval of close relatives. This concern can have a very bad influence on parenting. It keeps parents edgy and anxious. "Am I doing it right—what will others think?" Especially frequent is the outsider who has one simple solution to all parent-child problems: punishment of some kind.

Parents who decide to learn to use their heads more and their hands less in guiding their children often open themselves to criticism and slurs from other adults. It takes a lot of courage for parents to admit they are not perfect, that they didn't come equipped by instinct with all the answers, and that they are seeking more intelligent, effective and kindly methods of child rearing than many parents have been able to use to date.

25. Concern Over Spouse's Actions:

Suppose, after studying the Practical Parenting approach, you find yourself sold on the ideas, but your husband or wife rejects the whole thing as a bunch of nonsense. What then? Where does that leave you?

Actually, without any cooperation whatever from your mate, you can do a great deal of good for your children. Think how much better off they will be having at least one parent deal with them rationally in a manner that encourages their emotional growth.

Example: Father is too strict with his child. Mother resists the impulse to tell him how wrong he is. She doesn't try to make up to the child to offset the father's harsh behavior. She knows if she does interfere she:

• Prevents father and child from learning to work things out and learning how to get along with each other:

• Teaches the child to come hurrying to her when he fails to get along with others, thus depriving him of chances to learn to solve his own problems:

• Angers the father by her constant challenge to his authority and methods. This may spur him into being even more harsh. It certainly blocks cooperation in the family.

26. Say What You Mean, Mean What You Say:

Time after time parents make demands or give orders on the spur of the moment without really meaning what they say or expecting their demands to be carried out. When a parent does this he is teaching his child not to pay attention to him. Also, this impractical parent actually is training his child to hesitate before complying, to test the parent to find out whether he is really serious. Practical parents are aware of this pitfall. So they strive for consistency. They say what they mean and mean what they say.

27. To Spank or Not to Spank:

Of all questions that arise about wise and unwise parenting procedures, this one seems to generate the most heated argument. But as pointed out before, punishment of any kind usually has some totally unwanted and unexpected results. Almost always there are sounder ways to deal with disciplinary problems—but it takes time, patience and sometimes the counsel of some professional person outside the family to recognize wiser approaches.

It's a safe bet that physical punishment should be kept to an absolute minimum. If the parent panics and spanks, however, probably not too much harm will be done, providing future everyday efforts are made to enrich the basic relationship. Also, when the parent loses his cool and resorts to physical communication, a sincere apology often works wonders in restoring good will and fostering closer parent-child cooperation.

28. Who Owns Gifts?

One of the most outrageous things parents do is buy their child a gift—and then try to dictate how he should use or take care of it. Usually the child senses the fact that the parent's present is not without conditions, that the parent really has only loaned the object rather than giving it to the child with no strings attached.

Is it any wonder, then, that children often respond by being careless or by being downright destructive of the gift? When the relationship between a parent and his child has soured, what better way to torment the parent than to destroy the parent's gift? Practical parents don't give gifts to a child without also giving the child absolute title as to their use.

29. Nutrition and Child Behavior:

More and more evidence is piling up that the kinds of food children eat can radically affect their moods and behavior. Our modern "civilized" diet is full of starches and refined sugars that burn up fast. Between frequent fill-ups, children who are allowed to have starchy, sugary diets often tend to become hungry, irritable and uncooperative. They may grow aggressive and difficult to handle, even when parents use parenting techniques that normally work well with most children.

Practical Parents see to it that their children's diets contain a maximum of natural foods, such as fresh fruits, milk, nuts, vegetables, eggs, cheese, fish and lean meat. They keep foods of doubtful nutritional value at a minimum.

30. Children Thrive on Order and Regularity:

For parents and children to get along well together, it seems necessary that certain family routines be set up that are acceptable to and followed by both. When household duties and ways of dealing with common problems of family living are established, everyone knows where he stands and what he is supposed to do. Thus uncertainty and confusion are reduced to a minimum.

But—the parent's own behavior is the real key to success in attaining family orderliness and regularity. Practical Parents consistently model (demonstrate) these traits, faithfully follow routines and schedules, calmly expect their children to do the same, and usually find their children are quite willing on the whole to fit themselves into the program.

Family planning sessions in which all household tasks, chores and schedules are considered, discussed and worked out have proved extremely useful. Yet, when a particular routine or schedule interferes with family welfare or seems to cause friction, it should be re-examined and a new agreement reached.

31. Parents Often Defeat the Real Reasons for Allowances:

Providing their child with the opportunity to learn how to use money wisely and responsibly—this is the basic value of parents giving a weekly allowance. Most parents advance their children a fixed weekly amount of money for treats, school lunches, petty expenses and savings. As time goes on and financial requirements increase, the allowance is increased.

Some parents however, in their desire to punish the child for some infraction, will cut off their child's allowance. But is this parenting tactic really practical? When they deprive the child of his allowance, at the same time aren't they also depriving him of his means for learning money management?

Aren't they also showing the child that the allowance actually belongs to them and not the child? If so, what does this do to the child's attitude toward money and the prudent use of it?

Another thought: When these parents themselves behave foolishly (as most parents on occasion do) do they penalize themselves by shutting off their share of the family income? Of course not. What does their child learn from this double standard?

32. Regular Family Meetings:

Regular group discussions of family plans and concerns provide an extremely effective method for training children in decision-making and taking personal responsibility. Such meetings, preferably held at least weekly, give each family member a chance to voice his opinions, reveal his needs and ask questions. They help everyone in the family learn to have concern for the welfare of everyone. Discussion should center around "what we can do to prevent or solve problems." For meetings to work, each member must feel free to express his ideas, no matter how impractical-sounding they may appear to others.

Family meetings will flop—and deserve to—if parents use them as just another chance to tell children what to do. A further risk is that such meetings can turn into occasions where everyone gripes about the misdeeds of everybody else. Parents who dare to let their children take part in family meetings and decisions tell of improved agreement, cooperation and harmony. But sometimes it takes a good deal of patient keeping at it to get results.

33. Family Funtime:

Life in so many families is grim and joyless. Often it seems as though the only time parents and children talk is when things are going wrong. About the only thing family members do together is fight. What a tragedy! Playing together, sharing interests, getting to know one another during light-hearted times is almost a lost art. Fortunately, parents who decide to forego nagging, scolding, preaching and continually watching for misbehavior to correct have a good chance to change the scene. When they show as much interest in and learn to speak to their children as considerately as they do their friends, the children start *being* friends.

34. Parents Grow in Discussion Groups:

Merely listening to an expert, reading a book or making New Year's resolutions usually accomplish little in helping parents improve their parenting performance. What many parents seem to need is the encouragement, mutual support, shared experiences and common focus on the task of learning more about successful child rearing that can best be obtained in small study-discussion groups for parents.

Check around in your community. Find out whether such groups already exist. If so, join one. If there are none yet, it usually isn't too difficult to get one started among your friends, PTA or fellow church members.

Practical Parenting Publications makes available study-discussion plans for small groups of parents who can benefit more from a cooperative study approach than from going it alone.

Words and Actions That Encourage

One of the tragedies of our society is its emphasis on using discouragement and punishment as control methods, not only for children but for adults as well. For some reason, we have adopted the strange idea that the way to make people do better is through making them feel worse.

Following are some words, communication door openers, facial expressions and physical contacts that build children up—make them feel O.K.—instead of tearing them down. They can be tangible demonstrations that we care for them. Children who believe they are cared for seldom pose many serious behavior problems. They care in return.

It usually is remarkably revealing for a parent to check himself against the following words and actions to see how he rates as a builder of self-worth and self-esteem in his children.

Words That Stimulate Cooperation
Good, I agree, I see, Exactly, Please, Fine, O.K., Great, Oh, Really, Groovy, That's right, Thank you, Good idea, Very clever, Excellent, I'll buy that, I understand, I like that, You don't say, You did, huh, How considerate, I'm proud of you, I'm glad, Would you help me, Fine job, I'm happy.

Conversation "Door-openers"
Tell me about it, I'd like to hear about it, Tell me more, please, Want to talk about it, Let's discuss it, Let's hear your side, Shoot, I'm listening, Sounds like you got troubles, Seems pretty important to you, Tell me the whole story.

Facial Expression That Tell the Child He's O.K.
Smiling, Winking, Nodding head, Laughing, Wrinkling nose, Giggling, Looking interested, Grinning in friendly fashion.

Nearnesses That Tell the Child He's O.K.
Walking together, Sitting down beside, Talking-listening, Just visiting, Eating together, Playing games together, Solving a problem together, Going to a movie together.

Physical Contacts That Tell the Child He's O.K.
Sitting (holding) on lap, Patting back, shoulder, Stroking arm, Shaking hand, Petting, Fondling, Hugging, Touching, Holding hand, Nuzzling, Kissing, Embracing.

Five Myths That Sabotage Practical Parenting

1. That parents should have and must always get what they want when they want it (such as instant obedience) without needing to win their children's cooperation and good will.
   FACT   Parents who are considerate, friendly and patient with their children usually are for more successful than parents who demand instant results.

2. That children must be perfect, should never make mistakes, should never get in mean moods, should always be good, mannerly and thoroughly capable.
   FACT   No one is perfect. Parents and children alike are fallible persons, who often make mistakes in judgment and behavior.

3. That critizing, nagging, scolding, lecturing and becoming hostile toward children will change the children for the better and make them learn to cooperate.
   FACT   Such control methods seldom work, often backfire and result in children being even less willing to cooperate with and please their parents.

4. That children are born uncooperative, with a built-in determination to defy and rebel against parental authority.
   FACT   Children learn what they live. For the most part, their behavior reflects back the treatment given them by their parents. Example: Sassy children have sassy parents; impatient parents produce impatient children; cooperative, kindly parents rear cooperative, kindly children.

5. That children are to blame for their parent's feelings of anxiety, frustration and anger.
   FACT   Nobody makes anybody feel that way. We blame others, including children, when we refuse to accept our own personal responsibilities, when we do not want to take the time and make the effort necessary to achieve our wishes.

   AND the sad truth is: Parents who themselves have been taught to believe these myths, to have their unrealistic assumptions, teach their children also to have them. And the myths are handed down through the generations.

6
Coping with
Your Children's Misbehavior

Your single parent family probably faces some situations that are unique: however, many may be similar to those experienced by other families. In this section of the book several of the most common child rearing problems faced by single parents will be discussed. In your unique situation you may be able to relate to several of the examples or maybe none at all. You may agree with some of the suggested solutions or disagree totally. The important thing is that you learn how to utilize encouragement, consequences, and the family council in resolving your child rearing problems. If you disagree with a suggested solution, ask yourself "how would I handle that?" Or, if you have situations that are not discussed, write them on a piece of paper and use the techniques presented to help in resolving them. The examples are presented here only as suggestions; you and your children must decide the best solutions for your family.

Allowances

Billy, age 11, and his 8 year old sister, Martha, receive their allowance every Sunday. Somehow each week the children seem to run out of money and ask mother to give them additional funds. Mother usually feels sorry for them and as she gives them the money says "but this is the last time."

Money tends to be scarce in most families, especially single parent families, and can present many problems. It is important to realize the purpose of an allowance. Allowances are used to enable children to learn how to manage money. The allowance should not be used to bribe the children to do chores around the house or to achieve good grades in school.

In the situation with Billy and Martha, mother should explain to the children on Sunday when she gives them the allowance that it is up to them how they want to spend their money, but they should remember that no additional money will be forthcoming until next Sunday. If the children ask for additional money, mother should simply say, "You will get your allowance on Sunday."

The advantage to this approach to allowances is that the children learn to be responsible for their money and also learn to make decisions on how to spend their money. Mother should not get involved in what they should or should not buy. This would only create further problems and certainly deprive the children of deciding what to buy.

Bedtime

Susan, age 5, would always find reasons for mother to keep coming back in the room after being tucked in bed. Susan would yell to mother and say she was thirsty, needed to be covered up, or just wanted to talk. Mother would usually keep going back and giving Susan what she wanted, although she would become increasingly annoyed.

Based on the information, Susan's mistaken goal was probably attention. Mother and Susan should talk about the bedtime situation and agree on what routine will be followed. This discussion should take place at some time other than when Susan is getting ready for bed. Part of the bedtime routine should include ample opportunity for mother and Susan to talk, read, or engage in some other activity that they might select. Usually this activity takes place after Susan is ready for bed. If Susan is not ready for bed by the designated time, the activity will have to wait until the next night. Mother should also explain to Susan that once in bed, she will not return to her room and will see her in the morning. If Susan complains (and she probably will) mother should not return to the bedroom. As soon as Susan realizes that this means of trying to get mother's attention is useless, the behavior will stop. It is extremely important that mother be consistent in following the bedtime routine that is established.

Bedwetting

Fred, age 6, would frequently wet his bed at night and father would get furious. Usually Fred would get a spanking and be told that he should be ashamed of himself.

Bedwetting is not an uncommon problem in most families. In single parent families a child may develop into a bedwetter as a reaction to the loss of one of the parents. In helping a bedwetting child, the parent should not ridicule or scold because this only reinforces the problem and can affect the child's self-concept. Instead, the parent should be supportive and let the child assume responsibility for removing the bedding and, if the child is old enough, help with washing the soiled linen and remaking the bed. By making the child responsible for the behavior, it is unlikely that a mistaken goal of attention, power, or revenge is involved. On mornings when the bed is dry, the parent could make an encouraging comment such as, "You must be pleased about the dry bed!"

If the bedwetting persists, the single parent should have the child checked by a doctor for a physical problem; however, you may want to treat it as a behavior problem first.

Brushing Teeth

Four year old Amy refused to brush her teeth before bed. Mother would alternate between threats and bribes, both to no avail. Finally mother would scold Amy and send her to bed.

This is a fairly common problem and one in which logical consequences can be effectively used. The first step would be to discuss the situation with Amy and find out how she thinks the problem might be resolved. If she makes a reasonable suggestion, try it and see if it works. If no reasonable suggestions are made, mother could recommend something like "If you eat sweets and your teeth are not brushed, you will probably develop cavities. Therefore, candy and other sweets will have to be avoided until your teeth are being brushed on a regular basis."

Another approach to this problem would be to make sure that a routine for getting ready for bed is established and, if time remains before bedtime, mother and Amy could enjoy some activity. This activity might be reading a story, putting puzzles together, watching TV, or some other enjoyable project. However, if Amy is not ready at the appropriate time, mother would simply not have time for those activities. Getting ready could include such things as brushing teeth, putting on night clothes, and setting out the clothes to be worn the next day.

Child Abuse

Mother tried very hard to cope with the many problems since the divorce; however, sometimes she would seem to lose control. Three year old Lucy would not listen when told to do things. Mother would warn her and sometimes start slapping her. On a few occasions Lucy had to be treated by a doctor for the bruises.

Lucy's mother might be experiencing the anxiety and frustration resulting from the responsibilities of parenting alone. Most single parents are able to handle the responsibilities, even though it may not be easy. Other parents are unable to cope and use their children as an outlet for their frustration. These individuals should seek professional help to learn how to deal with the pressures that are facing them. A good starting point would be at the nearest mental health center.

Child Care

Since Mary's husband was killed in an automobile accident she has been forced to return to her career as a nurse. In order for Mary to work she has to put Mark, age 4, and Marcia, age 2 ½, in a day care center. When Mary drops them off at the center, they cry and beg her not to leave them.

Children frequently do not like to be left at a day care center and, in this situation, there are some additional considerations. The children may fear that their mother will leave them and not come back (which may be how they perceive the death of their father). Also, the mother may be experiencing guilt feelings about not being able to take care of the children herself.

The important thing to remember in this situation is that mother must return to work. She has no choice if the family is going to survive financially. Therefore, any guilt feelings are really non-productive and mother should face the reality that she must work and not feel guilty about leaving the children under the care of someone else. She should also remember that it is not the quantity of time that parents spend with their children that is important; but, rather the quality of the time with them.

In this specific case, mother could talk to the children at a time other than when she is leaving them at the center. She might tell them that she would rather be able to spend time with them; however, she must go to work so they can have food, clothes, and other things they need. Also, she could say that when she leaves them at the center this does not mean she does not love them, but simply that she must go to work. So tomorrow when they get to the center, she will give them each a kiss and say "Have a nice day." and then go to work.

It is important that mother follow through with what she said. Even though it might be difficult, she should not spend much time saying "good-bye" and allowing time for the guilt feeling to grow. The children will soon learn that they do not have a choice regarding staying at the day care center and accept the situation.

Disinterested Parent

Seana and David had been waiting for their father to come and take them to the zoo. He had promised he'd pick them up at one o'clock and now it is past two. The children are feeling disappointed and want to know why their father didn't come like he promised.

Unfortunately, the parents without custody of the children may have only minimal interest in visiting their children. The parent with custody has to deal with the children's disappointment. If you are unable to get your former spouse to see how important the visits are to the children and how hurt they feel when rejected, you may have to reevaluate how important the visits are when compared to the feelings of rejections they frequently experience.

Even though you may feel bitter toward your former spouse, the best thing you can do is help your children understand that they are loved and not at fault. You can identify with their hurt feelings, but point out the many people who love them (i.e., grandparents, aunts and uncles, friends), and try to find adults whom they can use as role models of how men and women should interact with children.

Disturbance While Driving

On numerous occasions mother narrowly missed having an accident when she tried to get Barry and Virginia to quiet down so she could concentrate on driving the car. No matter what she said the noise continued.

There are several approaches to this problem. One would be for mother to simply pull over to the side of the road (if traffic conditions would allow) and wait until it is quiet. If the children ask why she stopped, a reply like "I'm waiting until the noise quiets down so it will be safe to drive" would be appropriate. Note that mother is not trying to determine who caused the noise and blame any individual, but is treating every one the same. Usually this technique will be effective and it is common for the children to try and quiet each other down so they can get moving again. This approach can be done by the parent without having to yell, scream, or even lose her temper.

Another approach is to train the children by using activities they like. For example, mother might be taking the children for an ice cream cone, but when it gets too noisy she simply turns around and goes home. A statement like "maybe next time it will be quiet enough for us to get all the way to the store" would be sufficient. It is important to take the children places quite frequently so that they will learn appropriate traveling behavior. Unfortunately, most parents do not take time for training and the problem presents itself when they have to be some place by a certain time.

Dressing

Kelly, age 5, would not get dressed in the morning and mother would have to coax, threaten, bribe and anything she could think of because Kelly had to be dropped off at Kindergarten on her way to work.

This situation demonstrates how children can keep their parents busy with non-productive behavior. There are several things that Kelly's mother could do but the first step would be to talk with Kelly at a pleasant time (not when she is getting dressed in the morning) about the problem. Mother could start with something like "It seems the last few mornings you haven't been dressed when it is time for us to leave. What do you think we should do?" Possibly Kelly can come up with an idea that mother would feel comfortable about trying. If not, mother could tell Kelly what she will do in the morning. This might include not reminding Kelly about the need for her to get dressed and that they will leave for school at 8 A.M. and she can choose whether she would like to go with her night clothes on or get dressed. This might seem a bit harsh, but by making it the child's responsibility to get dressed and mother not giving her inappropriate attention, the misbehavior will normally stop very soon. If mother is somewhat apprehensive about the possibility that Kelly might really not get dressed for school, she could put some clothes in the car the night before. In most situations, however, the child will be dressed. It goes without saying that when Kelly is dressed, or shows improvement in her ability to dress herself, mother should make sure that encouragement is given.

Another possibility might be that if Kelly usually gets up and watches cartoons or some other enjoyable activity instead of getting dressed, it would be appropriate to tell Kelly that after she has completed her work (i.e., getting dressed) she could watch TV until it was time for school. If she is watching TV and still is not dressed, mother could simply unplug the TV and need not go into any lengthy explanations.

Fighting

Ten year old Sheila and her seven year old brother, Brian, would fight constantly. The fights would usually be so loud that mother would have to go in to settle the argument. Usually she scolded Sheila because she was older and should know better.

Fighting among siblings is not uncommon and will probably continue to some degree even after corrective action is taken. However, what mother must learn to do is keep herself out of playing "referee" for the children's fights. Rather than try to find who started the fight she could treat both individuals the same. If the fight is over a toy or game, that item could be removed until the children can play together. If the fight is taking place in the living room while you are watching TV, you could simply ask that they go outside until the fight is settled, or go to their rooms until they can behave appropriately. In other words, as a parent you should not have to be disturbed by their fights. However as long as you take responsibility for settling the children's fights they will keep coming to you. When the children realize it is their responsibility to get along, they will have fewer fights.

Former Spouse Remarries

Mark and Anne refuse to visit their father. In the past they always looked forward to going but since he has remarried the children would rather stay at home.

Frequently children who have managed to establish a good relationship with their non-custodial parent are shaken by a remarriage. They may seem angry or rejected and refuse to visit. It is important for you not to coax them to accept their stepparent, but be supportive when their feelings change and they want to reestablish their visitation schedule.

A stepparent can be an advantage to your children because another adult will be caring about them. At first the children may complain that the stepparent is too strict, unfair, or just does things differently. Children will establish a unique relationship with each adult and a stepparent is no exception. In the meantime it is important not to criticize the stepparent and, above all, do not quiz the children on what the stepparent is like. Remember, you are their custodial parent, and you are not being replaced. Be grateful that your children have another individual who cares about them.

Household Responsibilities

Sarah, age 14, has a room that appears to qualify for disaster aid, with clothes, coke glasses, and candy wrappers all over the floor; Pete, age 10, refuses to take out the trash on a regular basis, and the kitchen is in desperate need of some Lysol spray.

Sound familiar? These situations and numerous others present themselves in almost every single parent (and two parent) family. Many parents choose to deal with these problems in isolation; however, it is usually more effective to establish guidelines that pertain to most of the household responsibilities.

The first step would be to discuss the situation with the children probably at a family council meeting. Get as many suggestions as possible on what can be done to insure that the jobs are completed on time. If the children come up with some reasonable idea, give it a try and if the problem still exists the topic can be discussed again.

A common solution is to establish a day and time by which the jobs are to be done (i.e., Saturday morning). If the jobs are not completed, then no other activities will be started. This might mean no television, trip to the store, or going over to a friend's house. When the jobs are completed, then the children can participate in other activities. By using this approach the parent does not have to remind or coax the children; either the jobs are finished, or they are not. You should be careful not to impose a double standard, which means you should also have your jobs completed by the assigned time!

Living Together Arrangement

Jeanette and her five year old daughter, Marlene, had been living alone for about three years since the divorce. Recently, Jeanette has been dating Gary and they are strongly considering living together as a way of saving money by maintaining only one household.

This situation is becoming much more common in our society; however, there are several considerations besides the financial one. In making her decision Jeanette should seek answers to questions like: Am I doing this out of loneliness, or do I really love Gary? If the arrangement does not work, how do I get him to move out?; and Can I cope with the opinions my relatives and friends might have?

The most important questions, however, center around Marlene. What effect would Gary moving in have on her? Would she view him as a threat to her relationship with mother? Would he be considered her father, friend or uncle? How would she explain him to her friends and teachers at school?

It is probably obvious that there is no pat answer to this situation. However, care should be taken to determine not only the effect the relationship will have on you, but also your child. Even small children are aware of what is going on around them and learn to develop values from the modeling of adults.

Mealtime

Jeff, age 5, has always been a picky eater. His mother, a nurse, would coax him to eat all his food which sometimes took almost an hour. Mother felt it was extremely important that Jeff eat a balanced meal.

Eating problems are usually associated with the importance the single parent places on eating. Nurses and dieticians usually have a great deal of difficulty with their children not eating simply because a balanced meal is so important to them. In families where the parents really do not care if the children eat or not, there is usually no problem. The children cannot use eating habits as a source of attention or power in their relationship with their parents.

In Jeff's situations, mother could simply say "It is up to you if you want to eat or not; however, there will be no snacks until the next meal." Mother could eat her meal and when she finishes could simply clear her dishes off the table and go read the paper. Jeff, at that point, would probably either finish his meal, because mother is obviously not going to coax or nag him, or get up and leave the table too. In which case mother could also remove Jeff's dishes from the table. Usually, after this approach has been used a few times, Jeff will be eating a healthy meal simply because there is nothing to be gained by not eating.

Out-of-Town Parent

Jerry tells you how much he misses his mother since you separated and she has moved several hundred miles away to find work. He wishes he could visit her, but you explain it would be too expensive.

When the parents are living in different cities, the typical arrangement is that the child visits the non-custodial parent less frequently but for longer periods of time. During these long separations you can encourage the child to write or phone when feeling lonely. It is important for both parents to reassure the child that they love him and are not angry with him no matter which parent he is living with at the time.

Remarriage

Harriet has been a widow for five years and Sam has asked her to marry him. Margo, her twelve year old only child, says "If you marry him, I am going to run away. Who do you love, him or me?"

It appears that Harriet has a dilemma: Does she choose Sam or Margo? From Margo's point of view she is dead serious about her ultimatum. This situation would suggest that Margo is a spoiled child and mother has catered to her demands, possibly feeling sorry for her because of the death of her father.

What should Harriet do? If she loves Sam and feels that their marriage would succeed, then she should probably go ahead. This does not mean that Margo's feelings should be ignored. Mother should talk with her about how she plans to marry Sam and this in no way means she loves Margo any less. Care should be taken to avoid arguments with Margo. Harriet should state her views and listen to Margo's feelings. After the marriage, Sam should not be forced on Margo as her father. Let the two of them establish their own relationship. Forcing Margo to call Sam "Father" might only lead to further resentment by Margo.

Single parents should not allow themselves to be pressured into remarrying. While this is not the case with Harriet and Sam, it happens entirely too frequently. Friends and parents with the best of intentions some times push single parents into marriages. Likewise in some single parent families, the children are the one's pushing their parent to remarry. However, under no circumstances should the single parent remarry until he or she feels ready.

School Work

John is in sixth grade and failing most of his subjects. Mother had a conference with John's teachers, and they said the major problem was his reluctance to do homework, and they had no choice but to give him a zero on the assignments. Mother tried to force John to do his homework and made sure each assignment was finished. However, at the next grading period John was still failing because of not handing in his homework. When his mother questioned him, John replied, "You can make me do my homework but you can't make me turn it in at school."

Mother and John are involved in a power struggle, and the harder mother pressures him regarding the school work the more the struggle will escalate.

Your role as a parent is to support your children in their school work and offer them encouragement at every possible opportunity. In this way the children will gain confidence in being able to do the work and their ability to accomplish tasks. However, if you take responsibility for your children's school work, they will be denied this opportunity to improve their self-confidence.

As a family you may want to decide on certain times to study; however, the amount of time should be reasonable. Children need time to relax and have fun just like adults. School work is important, but it should be kept in perspective with regard to the development of the total individual.

Television

Father would lose his temper when thirteen year old Joe and eleven year old Ed would fight over which television show to watch. Each would take turns switching the channel until a major disturbance took place. Father would come into the room yelling, give each one a swat on the behind and send them to their room.

There is no doubt that television is the source of many family problems. In this case all father would have to do would be to turn off the television and say "when you two decide what you are going to watch, you can turn the set back on." This action by father places the responsibility on the two boys to decide how they are going to handle the problem. If the boys again fight after the set is turned on, father could go back and shut the set off and say "I can see you were unable to solve your problem. Maybe tomorrow you will be able to agree on what you are going to watch."

Notice that father would be taking action and talking very little. The boys would soon learn that it is much more advantageous to cooperate than to fight.

Visitation Schedule

Paul and Debbie were recently divorced after five years of marriage. Debbie received custody of their two children, Dee age 4 and Susan age 2; however, both parents felt it was extremely important for the girls to see their father.

There are really no pat answers in establishing a visitation schedule. Some general guidelines might include scheduling shorter more frequent visits with younger children and longer, possibly extended, visits with older children. It is extremely important that the custodial parent clue the other parent in on the children's typical daily routine so that there will be as much consistency as possible.

The custodial parents should also realize that even if they do not get along well with their former spouse, the children should not be prejudiced by your feelings. Let them establish and maintain their own feelings. And, remember, the other person is as much the children's parent as you are!

7
Resources for the Single Parent

There are many publications, support groups and other resources available to single parents and their children. Reading about how other single parents were able to cope with their situation can be very helpful. Publications designed for your children can aid them in better understanding their feelings and in coping with the everyday concerns of a child in a single parent family.

A comprehensive listing of material available to you and your children is presented in this chapter. Topics included are: Separation and Divorce Reading List; Separation and Divorce: Resources—Groups—Publications; Separation and Divorce: Annotated Bibliography of Selected Literature for Children and Teens; Widowed Reading List; and Single Father's Reading List. These materials were prepared by the PWP Information Center and are reprinted by permission of Parents Without Partners, Inc.

Separation and Divorce Reading List

*Bohannan, Paul, DIVORCE AND AFTER, Garden City, NY: Doubleday, 1970. Pb.
> Excellent collection of articles analyzing the divorce process, legal, cultural and emotional. Includes recommendations for change.

Despert, J. Louise, CHILDREN OF DIVORCE, Garden City, NY: Doubleday, 1962. Pb.
> Says that children fare better when parents in deep conflict divorce rather than continue marriage. Points out ways of safeguarding children. Somewhat traditional views, but a classic.

*Edwards, Marie and Eleanor Hoover, THE CHALLENGE OF BEING SINGLE, Los Angeles: J.P. Tarcher, Inc., 1974. Pb (available from PWP Int., $1.50).
> Practical guide for living a full life as a single person freed from self limiting expectations of finding completeness from a magical "one and only" partner.

Eisler, Riane, T., DISSOLUTION: NO-FAULT DIVORCE, MARRIAGE AND THE FUTURE OF WOMEN. McGraw Hill, 1977.
> Outlines changes in divorce and marriage from point of view of equality between the sexes. Personal divorce checklist and discussion of marriage contracts.

Forman, Lynn, GETTING IT TOGETHER, New York: Berkeley Publ. Co., 1974. Pb.
> A practical and positive guide for women that focuses on becoming your own person again (or for the first time). Particularly good on the parent child relationship.

Fuller, Jan, SPACE: THE SCRAPBOOK OF MY DIVORCE, New York: Arthur Fields Books, 1973.
> Diary of a woman's thoughts and experiences for several months after her divorce. Heavily polished writing with misty color photo-illustrations.

*Recommended.

*Gardner, Richard, THE BOYS AND GIRLS BOOK ABOUT DIVORCE, New York: Science House, 1970. Pb (Available from PWP Int., $1.25).
    An excellent guide to help children understand and deal with their parents' divorce. Valuable for parents as well.

Gardner, Richard, THE PARENTS BOOK ABOUT DIVORCE, Doubleday, 1977.
    Psychoanalytically oriented discussion in depth of possible problems with children. Warnings on using children as weapons and healthy visitation guidelines.

*Gettleman, Susan and Janet Markowitz, THE COURAGE TO DIVORCE, New York: Simon and Schuster, 1974. Pb.
    A thorough analysis of anti-divorce forces and the damaging myths about divorce in this society. Suggests reform of marriage as well as of divorce. Emphasis on opportunities for personal growth, but not a guide book.

Hallett, Kathryn, A GUIDE FOR SINGLE PARENTS, Millbrae, CA: Celestial Arts, 1973.
    Transactional analysis for people in crisis.

Hensley, J. Clark, HELP FOR SINGLE PARENTS, Jackson, MS: Christian Action Commission, 1973.
    A very human but more conservative guide to divorce, based in Christian theology.

Hirsch, Barbara B., DIVORCE: WHAT A WOMAN NEEDS TO KNOW, Chicago: Henry Regnery Co., 1974. Pb.
    Discussion of legal aspects of divorce including custody, financial matters, courtroom hearings. Briefly considers the impact of "no-fault" divorce on women, but primarily concerned with divorce under traditional fault laws. Oriented toward middle class.

Hunt, Morton, THE WORLD OF THE FORMERLY MARRIED, New York: McGraw-Hill, 1966. Pb.
    Describes the subculture of the separated and divorced. A classic, out of print, but available at some libraries. Look for Mr. Hunt's new book, soon to be published.

Kelleher, Stephen J., DIVORCE AND REMARRIAGE FOR CATHOLICS? Garden City: NY, Doubleday, 1973. Pb.
    A provocative analysis of the Catholic Church's position on divorce, questions as to its validity, and suggestions for a different approach.

Kessler, Sheila, THE AMERICAN WAY OF DIVORCE: PRESCRIPTIONS FOR CHANGE, Chicago: Nelson-Hall, 1975.
    Analyzes individual and societal aspects of divorce, recommends changes in both areas, discusses "dissolution training."

*Krantzler, Mel, CREATIVE DIVORCE, New York: M. Evans & Co., 1974. Pb.
    Very good discussion of the divorce process, with a description of divorce counseling. Emphasis is on maximizing this opportunity for personal growth.

Mindey, Carol, THE DIVORCED MOTHER, New York: McGraw-Hill, 1969.
    Practical, although "unliberated," guide to all aspects of divorce, with emphasis on personal growth. Particularly good sections on children and psychotherapy.

Napolitane, Catherine & Vicoria Pellegrino, LIVING AND LOVING AFTER DIVORCE, New York: Rawson Associates, 1977.
    Popularly written discussions about practical aspects of divorce, sex, dating for women. Author is founder of divorce organization for women.

*Recommended.

Singleton, Mary Ann, LIFE AFTER MARRIAGE, New York: Stein and Day, 1974.
Practical and candid guide for women, emphasizing development of identity and potential. Especially good in discussing relationships with men.

Steinzor, Bernard, WHEN PARENTS DIVORCE, New York: Pantheon, 1969. Pb.
A guide for parents in helping children through divorce and afterwards. Does not demand the pretense of affection between ex-spouses. Promotes openness in relationships.

Weiss, Robert S., MARITAL SEPARATION, New York: Basic Books, 1975.
Helpful *verbatim* reports from separated people with discussion. Most useful for those undergoing separation, especially those who were "left." Gives perspectives on what is normal after loss and disruption of intimate relationships. Many will not agree with his prescription to find a new attachment.

Wheeler, Michael, NO-FAULT DIVORCE, Boston: Beacon Press, 1974. Pb.
Excellent analysis of our divorce laws and the movement toward no-fault divorce. Provides extensive discussion and documentation of advantages, disadvantages and gaps in traditional, new and proposed legislation, with a look at the politics of reform. Sensitive to needs of both men and women.

WOMEN IN TRANSITION: A FEMINIST HANDBOOK ON SEPARATION AND DIVORCE, New York: Charles Scribner's Sons, 1975. Pb.
Feminist oriented comprehensive guide written by women who have experienced separation and divorce. All inclusive bibliography and resources lists.

Wrenn, Lawrence G., Ed., DIVORCE AND REMARRIAGE IN THE CATHOLIC CHURCH, New York: Newman Press, 1973.
A guide for Catholics.

Separation and Divorce
Resources—Groups—Publications

Parents Without Partners, Inc., 7910 Woodmont Avenue, Washington, D.C., 20014. With 130,000 members (1976), the largest organization devoted to single parents and their children. Educational materials, 900 Chapters, magazine.

North American Conference of Separated and Divorced Catholics, The Paulist Center, 5 Park Street, Boston, 02108. Recently expanding. Newsletter, $7/year.

MOMMA, P.O. Box 567, Venice, CA 90291. Program similar to PWP (smaller). The Sisterhood of Black Single Mothers, P.O. Box 155, Brooklyn, NY 11203. Has Newsletter (25¢ a copy), support programs, day care, meetings, bibliographies. Hoping to expand to other areas of the country.

Women in Transition, 4634 Chester Avenue, Philadelphia, PA 14143. (215) 724–9511. Excellent programs and publications, holds small group discussions, has telephone counseling. Is funded.

KNOW, Inc., P.O. Box 86031, Pittsburgh, PA 15221. Publishes articles and training manuals for support group facilitators to explain Women in Transition model. "What to Look for in a Lawyer." (35¢)

George F. Doppler, Coordinator, National Council of Marriage and Divorce Law Reform and Justice Organizations. P.O. Box 60, Broomall, PA 19008. Has list of organizations for men, fathers' rights.

Family Mediation Center, Inc., 291 Lindbergh Dr., NW, Atlanta, GA 30305. A private center, but the principles used could be a worthwhile community project.

Displaced Homemakers Alliance, 4223 Telegraph Ave., Oakland, CA 94609. Interested in women returning to work.

CATALYST, 14 E. 60th Street, New York, NY 10022. Non-profit organization working directly with women, local resource groups and the like that are concerned with women and employment.

Creative Divorce National Counseling Center, 818 Fifth Avenue, San Rafael, CA 94901. Groups for adults, children, research, education, training center for divorce counseling.

YMCA's have single parent groups. Described in *Circulator,* Vol. 6, Fall, 1975. Mrs. Charlotte Himber, Editor, 291 Broadway, New York, NY 10007.

Many local Commissions for Women have useful publications and/or conduct groups for women, single parents.

The Single Parent Resource Center, 3896 24th Street, San Francisco, CA 94114. Publications, referrals. Counseling, workshops. (415) 821–7058.

Local Social Service Agencies of PTA's conduct single parent groups.

Agencies, Adult Education Services have separation/divorce seminars and parenting groups.

Many colleges and Universities conduct groups for single parents, some in cooperation with local PWP Chapters.

Big Brothers of America, 910 Mall Building, 4th and Chestnut, Philadelphia, PA 19106. Local agencies work with fatherless boys.

CENTER FOR CHILDREN IN FAMILY CRISIS, 1603 Arrott Bldg., 401 Wood St., Pittsburgh, PA 15222. (412) 281–0552. Creative program for children and parents. Focus on changes of divorce.

Divorce and Marital Stress Clinic, 1925 N. Lynn St., Suite 800, Arlington, VA 22209. Walk in counseling, seminars, support groups. Good model for community or private divorce counseling project.

Single Parent Resource Center, 105 East 22nd Street, New York, NY 10010. New center for New York area.

Single Parent Program, Family Service of Santa Monica, 1539 Euclid Street, Santa Monica, CA 90904. Cooperates with UCLA in excellent single parent program, group meetings, seminar.

Parents and Child Care Resources, 1855 Folsom Street, San Francisco, CA 94103. Referral services, day care information hot-line.

Booklet: "Parents Are People" DHEW publication 74–48, 5600 Fishers Lane, Alcohol, Drug Abuse and Mental Health Administration, Rockville, MD 20852. Lists many group efforts to help parents, single parents (55¢).

The Single Parent, Journal of Parents Without Partners, Inc., 7910 Woodmont Avenue, Washington, D.C. 20014. $5.50/year 10 issues.

The Single Parent News, P.O. Box 5877, Santa Monica, CA 90405. Excellent new Newsletter, $3/year.

Consumer Survival Kit—Split Decision, Maryland Center for Public Broadcasting, Owings Mills, MD 21117. $1, has reprints of articles and comprehensive bibliography about divorce.

Newsletter: *Marriage and Divorce Today,* 2315 Broadway, New York, NY 10024.

Journal of Divorce, Haworth Press, 149 Fifth Avenue, New York, NY 10010.

Journal of Clinical Child Psychology, Summer, 1977: "Divorce—Its Impact Upon Children and Youth." $3, 1100 N.E. 13th, Oklahoma City, OK 73117.

Divorce Adjustment Institute, Dr. Joseph Federico, 708 Church St., Evanston, IL 60201. Seminars and group counseling program.

"Kids in the Middle," Ms. Kim Long, 226 S. Meramec, Suite 201, Clayton, MO 63105. Conducts group sessions with children of divorce.

Evergreen Developmental Center, Dr. Kenneth Magid, Director, P.O. Box 14, Evergreen, CO 80439. Group sessions for parent and children, with special emphasis on adjustments of children following divorce.

Public Affairs Pamphlets, 381 Park Avenue S., New York, NY 10016. Has booklets for 35¢ each on many subjects, including Divorce, One Parent Families, Losing a Loved One Through Death, Parenting.

The New Women's Survival Catalog, (Karen Grimstad and Susan Rennie, Coward, McCann and Geoghegan, 1973), contains a comprehensive listing of women's projects throughout the country.

SOLO, 1882 NW Broadway, Portland, OR 97232. Resource for single adults *and* children 6–12.

Ann Landers has listing of supportive groups and agencies in more than 800 cities where her column appears. Contact through newspaper.

Parents Without Partners, Inc., Information Center, 7910 Woodmont Avenue, Washington, D.C. 20014 has reading lists (separated and divorced, widowed, fathers, children's literature), pamphlets, child support information, and other materials.

Separation and Divorce: Annotated Bibliography of Selected Literature for Children and Teens

Recent books portraying children who are experiencing family changes due to divorce and adjusting to stepparents have become more plentiful. Reading about how others have handled similar situations can be helpful for your children, giving them perspective, awareness of some of their feelings, fears, or mistaken ideas, and suggesting ways to solve problems. Many children's books are helpful for parents, too . . . not just to read but also to use as a starting point in discussions. Honest communication about what is happening seems to help children learn coping skills and become more able to contribute to the effective functioning of the family—albeit a single parent family.

The following bibliography was prepared by the PWP Information Center and a representative of the Committee on Liaison with National Organizations Serving the Child of the American Library Association. Books for younger children are listed first. Following are books showing the approximate school grade, although children may vary in reading comprehension level. Last, nonfiction books for children, young adults and parents have been included.

Your children's librarian or school library can be helpful in finding these and other books for your particular situation.

Preschool and Beginning Readers	Adams, Florence, MUSHY EGGS. Putnam's, 1973. The story of a family managing well after divorce.
	Clifton, Lucile. EVERETT ANDERSON'S FRIEND. Holt, Rinehart & Winston, 1976. Everett's mother is angry because he lost his housekey. He thinks about what his father might have said if he had been there. Resolves positively.
F	Eichler, Margaret, MARTIN'S FATHER. Lollipop Power, 1971. A matter-of-fact presentation of daily life of a boy who lives with his father.
	Goff, Beth. WHERE IS DADDY? THE STORY OF A DIVORCE. Beacon Press, 1969. A little girl learns not to blame herself for her parents' divorce. Criticized for its super sad quality, it may be most useful in stimulating discussion of a young child's fears.
F	Kindred, Wendy. LUCKY WILMA. Dial Press, 1973. A loving father visits his young daughter every Saturday. Demonstrates that visitation, especially shared time rather than places, is something positive a youngster can count on.
	Lexau, Joan. EMILY AND THE KLUNKY BABY AND THE NEXT DOOR DOG. Dial Press, 1972. Emily's feelings of being neglected after her parents' divorce are finally resolved. Good messages for parents in this book.
	Pursell, Margaret Sanford. A LOOK AT DIVORCE. Lerner, 1976. Text and photographs describe changes children and parents may make following divorce. Generally positive attitudes. Pictures make it a good book to read and discuss with little ones.

F indicates Positive father-child relationship.

Rogers, Helen Spelman. MORRIS AND HIS BRAVE LION. McGraw-Hill, 1975.

Touching treatment of divorce for a young child, despite the unrealistic story ending which may give false hopes to a child who wishes his parents to reunite.

Surowiecki, Sandra. JOSHUA'S DAY. Lollipop Power, 1972.

Joshua is coping with living with his mother and going to a Day Care Center. Positive, specific book.

*
F

Thomas, Ianthe. ELIZA'S DADDY. Harcourt Brace Jovanovich, 1976.

The young heroine has feelings about father's remarriage that are eased by visiting his new "family." Jealousy and fears are resolved in this LET ME READ book.

Zindel, Paul. I LOVE MY MOTHER. Harper and Row, 1975.

A small boy's story about his single parent mother, who not only cooks but teaches him to kick a football.

BOOKS BY GRADE LEVEL

3rd-5th

Anker, Charlotte, LAST NIGHT I SAW ANDROMEDA, Walch, 1975.

Eleven year old Jenny discovers she really needn't try so hard to earn her divorced father's love and appreciation.

5th-9th

Alexander, Ann. TO LIVE A LIE. Atheneum, 1975.

Tale of a 12 year old who imagines herself unloved and unwanted by divorcing parents. She lies and fibs to give herself a new identity.

7th-up
T

Arundel, Honor. A FAMILY FAILING. Thomas Nelson, 1972.

A girl grows up after parents' separation and learns to view her parents as people independently from herself. Story set in Scotland.

4th-6th

Blue, Rose. A MONTH OF SUNDAYS. Franklin Watts, 1972.

Divorce and change do not mean disaster for 10 year old Jeffrey, who soon understands his parents must also readjust. Some stereotyped ideas regarding the role of women.

4th-7th
*

Blume, Judy. IT'S NOT THE END OF THE WORLD. Bradbury Press, 1972.

Karen and her sister cope with their feelings after divorce. Helpful for those experiencing similar situations.

5th-8th
F

Butterworth, W.E. Steve Bellamy. Little, Brown and Co., 1970.

After his mother and stepfather were killed in an auto accident, Steve goes to live with his father, whom he had never met. For children learning to accept new ways and new places.

5th-8th

Cleaver, Vera and Bill. ELLEN GRAE. Lippincott, 1967.

A girl survives the aftermath of her parents' divorce, even though she does not live with either of them. The divorce itself is not handled in this tale set in Appalachia.

F indicates Positive father-child relationship.
* indicates Recommended.
T indicates Young adult, IYC (PWP International Youth Council), Teen interests.

3rd-5th	Clymer, Eleanor. LUKE WAS THERE. Holt Rinehart & Winston, 1973.

It seemed that whenever Julius began to rely on an adult, something would go wrong. His father left, his mother was in the hospital and he must stay in a children's home. He develops a secure relationship with Luke, a social worker.

3rd-6th   Ewing, Kathryn. A PRIVATE MATTER. Harcourt Brace Jovanovich, 1975.

Marcy must give up her dream father, an elderly man next door, for the reality of her mother's second marriage. Tender story.

4th-9th   Green, Constance. A GIRL CALLED AL. Viking, 1969.

Alexandra is unhappy and finds her father's money for support is no substitute for his love. Useful if other books are read to give a more positive perspective.

4th-9th   Green, Constance. I KNOW YOU AL. Viking, 1975.

The sequel in which Al attends her father's wedding.

4th-9th   Gripe, Marie. THE NIGHT DADDY. Delacorte Press, 1971.

Mother works at night. The young heroine becomes friends with the baby sitter. A solution for this family.

6th-up
T

Holland, Isabelle. THE MAN WITHOUT A FACE. Lippincott, 1972.

A somewhat controversial story about a much divorced mother and her family. Charlie has quite a time adjusting, but is helped by his friendship with an older man.

6th-up
T
F

Holland, Isabelle. OF LOVE AND DEATH AND OTHER JOURNEYS. Lippincott, 1975.

After a nomadic existence with her mother, Meg learns her mother is dying and she must live with her father whom she does not remember. After a bad start, her relationship with him improves as both talk honestly about their feelings.

5th-9th   Hunter, Evan. ME AND MR. STENNER. Lippincott, 1976.

Abby is often very cruel as she grows to understand and to love her new stepfather. Includes the time of divorce for both parents and then the remarriage and honeymoon.

4th-7th   Jones, Cordelia. CAT CALLED CAMOUFLAGE. S.G. Phillips, 1971.

After finally beginning to adjust to her new home, Ruth began to suspect her parents might reconcile. She wanted that, but remembering the fights, she also feared it. There is very little frank discussion between parent and child.

6th-up
T

Klein, Norma. IT'S NOT WHAT YOU EXPECT. Pantheon, 1973.

A "liberated" family weathers dad's three month "absence."

4th-8th   Klein, Norma. TAKING SIDES. Pantheon, 1974.

Real people cope with separation after remarriage. Father is portrayed as a nurturing person. Avon Pb.

F indicates Positive father-child relationship.
T indicates Young adult, IYC (PWP International Youth Council), Teen interests.

5th-9th   Klein, Norma. MOM, THE WOLFMAN AND ME. Pantheon,
T   1972.

Brett and her mother, who has never been married, live a happy but non-traditional life. Brett brings to worry when her mother starts dating and may marry. Avon Pb.

5th-9th   Klein, Norma. WHAT'S IT ALL ABOUT? Dial Press, 1975.

Many complicated family changes confront a 10 year old girl, including a stepfather who leaves when an adopted sister joins the family.

2nd-4th   Lisker, Sonia. TWO SPECIAL CARDS. Harcourt Brace Jovanovich, 1976.

Young children adjust to their parents' divorce. Story portrays father visiting children and a loving mother in a realistic way.

2nd-4th   Madison, Winifred. MARINKA, KATINKA AND ME (SUSIE).
*   Bradbury Press, 1975.

Portrays friendship among three fourth grade girls whose non-traditional families are accepted as they are. Susie's father is dead, Marinka's parents are divorced and Katinka's father is in prison. Puts realistic problems, including divorce, in perspective.

3rd-6th   Mann, Peggy. MY DAD LIVES IN A DOWNTOWN HOTEL.
*   Doubleday, 1973.

Since both parents are careful to assure him they do not blame one another for their divorce, Joey concludes that *he* is the cause. Gradually Joey learns to face reality and cope with life as it is. Basis for an After School Special on ABC TV. Avon Pb.

6th-9th   Mazer, Harry. GUY LENNY. Delacorte Press, 1971, Dell Pb.

Twelve year old Guy lives with his father and rebels mightily when father wishes to remarry. His father decides that Guy should live with his mother, at least for a while. Harsh realities following divorce are portrayed in this book.

4th-9th   Mazer, Norma. I, TRISSY. Delacorte, 1971.
T

Trissy uses her typewriter to vent frustrations about her parents' divorce and problems brought on by her selfishness and unwillingness to understand her parents. Finally she begins to question her own identity and becomes better able to face these troubles.

5th-8th   McHargue, Georgess. STONEFLIGHT. Viking Press, 1975.
*

Janie suspected a divorce but no one would talk to her. She wished she were like the stone Griffon which "cannot be hurt." Through her uncle, she becomes included in family discussions of the problem.

6th-up   Naylor, Phyllis. NO EASY CIRCLE. Follet, 1972.
T

Teenagers whose parents have divorced will identify with the young girl in this story as she faces problems with her peers as well as her parents.

5th-up   Neville, Emily Cheney. GARDEN OF BROKEN GLASS. Dela-
T   corte, 1975.

* indicates Recommended.
T indicates Young adult, IYC (PWP International Youth Council), Teen interests.

Thirteen year old Brian grows in awareness of others as he finds ways to live despite an absent father and an alcoholic mother. Considered outstanding by the Child Study Association of America, Wel-Met Incorporated.

3rd-5th
*
F

Newfield, Marcia. A BOOK FOR JODAN. Atheneum, 1975.

Jodan, nine, doesn't believe her parents' reassurances of their love for her after their separation. Both parents work to promote her constructive adjustment, even though father lives across the country. Details an excellent, creative project for fathers.

4th-6th

Norris, Gunilla. LILLAN. Atheneum, 1968.

Many will identify with fears that mother's full time job will damage her relationship with her daughter. With mother's help, Lillan becomes more self-reliant and able to meet the needs of the situation.

5th-9th

Perl, Lila. THE TELLTALE SUMMER OF TINA C. Seabury Press, 1975.

Trying to untangle the confusing relationship of divorce and remarriage, Tina begins to understand her loved ones. Portrays positive, open relationships with both parents.

5th-up
*

Pevsner, Stella. A SMART KID LIKE YOU. Seabury Press, 1975.

A realistic view of some afteraffects of divorce. Nina finds her new Math teacher is her father's new wife. This was an After School TV Special.

5th-9th
T

Pfeffer, Susan Beth. MARLY THE KID. Doubleday & Co., 1975.

During her sophomore year, Marly acts courageously. She decides to live with her father instead of her mother and also refuses to tolerate insulting remarks from her History teacher. The step-mother is an even tempered, positive figure.

7th-up
T

Platt, Kin. THE BOY WHO COULD MAKE HIMSELF DIS-APPEAR. Chilton, 1968, Dell Pb. Also CHLORIS AND THE CREEPS.

These two stories are complicated, unusual and somewhat painful about young people coping with divorce and remarriage. There is partial resolution of extremely negative situations and behavior. Not for those actually experiencing the acute stages of loss.

5th-9th

Sachs, Marilyn. THE BEAR'S HOUSE. Doubleday, 1971.

Ghastly and emotional situations confront a young girl and her older brother who take responsibility for younger children and a mentally ill mother after father leaves. Painful to read, but value may lie in realizing that others have more terrible problems than you have.

5th-8th

Sheffield, Janet N. NOT JUST SUGAR AND SPICE. William Morrow and Co., 1975.

Lani is jealous, selfish and losing friends rapidly. Only to get rid of a domineering housekeeper does she decide to pull herself together, cooperate with her future stepfather, and help out while her mother is in the hospital.

F indicates Positive father-child relationship.
* indicates Recommended.
T indicates Young adult, IYC (PWP International Youth Council), Teen interests.

5th-9th   Smith, Doris. KICK A STONE HOME. Crowell, 1975.
*   After three years, Sara Jane still hopes her father will come
                 back. She hates visiting him and his new wife and has no one with
                 whom to share her feelings. Gradually, negativism and resentment
                 toward the remarriage soften. Positive portrayal of real people.

5th-8th   Synder, Zilpha Keatley. HEADLESS CUPID. Atheneum, 1971.
                      Fun and intrigue result when stepbrothers and sisters begin
                 adjusting to each other and to their new parents.

ALL AGES   Sitea, Linda. "Zachary's Divorce" in FREE TO BE ME. McGraw
*   Hill, 1974.
                      This entire book is an absolutely delightful look at children's
                 emotions and values aimed at self-acceptance. Zachary's story
                 about "his" divorce is simple, but captures the feelings of a small
                 boy.

7th-up   Stolz, Mary. LEAP BEFORE YOU LOOK. Harper & Row, 1972.
*   Dell Pb.
T   The young heroine lives with her mother and has difficulty
                 adjusting to her father's remarriage. A friend helps her to reconcile
                 her feelings.

5th-9th   Sullivan, Mary. BLUE GRASS IGGY. Nelson, 1975.
F   Iggy makes friends in the trailer camp where he lives with his
                 father.

6th-9th   Thorval, Kerstin. AND LEFFE WAS INSTEAD OF A DAD.
                 Bradbury Press, 1974.
                      Magnus' mother lives with Leffe, who becomes the dad that
                 Magnus always wanted. When Leffe began drinking again, there
                 was the chance that he would leave or break parole. An unusual
                 story with warmth and understanding, translated from the Swedish
                 original.

4th-6th   Warren, Mary Phraner. THE HAUNTED KITCHEN. West-
F   minster Press, 1976.
                      After the divorce, Dad decides to go back to school. He and his
                 three children move to Oregon and live in what appears to be a
                 haunted house. Children coping with reality and working cooper-
                 atively are portrayed.

5th-8th   Wolitzer, Hilma. OUT OF LOVE. Farrar, Straus & Giroux, 1976.
                      Two years after the divorce, Teddy is still scheming to reunite
                 her parents, through illness and by crusading to better her mother's
                 appearance. Rather superficial characterization, but emotions seem
                 genuine.

NONFICTION PUBLICATIONS FOR CHILDREN

These books are for readers about 4th grade and up, including *parents*.

*   Gardner, Richard. THE BOYS AND GIRLS BOOK ABOUT
                 DIVORCE. Science House, Inc., 1971. Bantam Pb.
                      The classic for children AND parents. Handles simply and di-
                 rectly the anxieties and reactions that children may experience.

F indicates Positive father-child relationship.
* indicates Recommended.
T indicates Young adult, IYC (PWP International Youth Council), Teen interests.

Gives children straight answers and practical suggestions about handling themselves and making the best of the situation. The cartoon illustrations are explicit, delightful, and enhance the message of the text. Much of the book could be read to younger children.

Hautzig, Esther. LIFE WITH WORKING PARENTS. Macmillan, 1976.

Practical hints for children for every day situations. Since routines may change after separation and divorce, it could be useful for single parent families. Individual families may wish to do things differently, but it can be used as a starting point for family discussions.

Kalb, Jonah and David Viscott. WHAT EVERY KID SHOULD KNOW. Houghton Mifflin Co., 1976.

Practical discussions which direct children trying to understand their feelings, inadequacies, relationships with parents and friends, and their parents' divorce. Includes a Bill of Rights For Kids . . . with corresponding responsibilities. Worthwhile for parents, too.

Leshan, Eda. WHAT MAKES ME FEEL THIS WAY? Macmillan, 1972.

In this little book, emotions are identified and discussed in terms that children can understand. A book for parents and children to read together.

Leshan, Eda. YOU AND YOUR FEELINGS. Macmillan, 1975.

A guide for young people to better understand their feelings and their relationships with others. A good book for junior high level.

*
T   Richards, Arlene and Irene Willia. HOW TO GET IT TO-GETHER WHEN YOUR PARENTS ARE COMING APART. David McKay, 1976.

This book gives examples of what young adults and teens may need to cope with during their parents' marital troubles, separation, divorce and after. The emphasis is on awareness of feelings, coping skills and reassurance that they are able to take responsibility for their own lives. The stories are forth-right, actual happenings that nearly everyone can identify with. That teens have choices in how they will allow parental troubles to affect them is refreshing and positive. The messages are not patronizing: "It doesn't matter so much what your problems are; what really counts is how you handle them."

*   Rosenbaum, Jean and Lutie McAuliffe. WHAT IS FEAR? AN INTRODUCTION TO FEELINGS. Prentice-Hall, 1972.

Clear and sensitive discussion of common fears, understanding them and handling them. Divorce is briefly touched on. Excellent for parents who want to better understand their children and why they do things.

---

* indicates Recommended.
T indicates Young adult, IYC (PWP International Youth Council), Teen interests.

Widowed Reading List

Caine, Lynn, WIDOW, William Morrow, 1974, Bantan Pb.
> Frank and moving account of a woman working her way through the first year of widowhood.

Grollman, Earl A., SUICIDE, Beacon Press, 1971.

Grollman, Earl A., TALKING ABOUT DEATH: A DIALOGUE BETWEEN PARENT AND CHILD, Beacon Press, 1976.
> Realistic suggestions to assist children in dealing with parental loss by death.

Grollman, Earl A., Ed., EXPLAINING DEATH TO CHILDREN, Beacon Press, 1967.
> Variety of articles of interest to those who work with widowed.

*Grollman, Earl A., LIVING WHEN A LOVED ONE HAS DIED, Beacon Press, 1977.
> From shock, suffering and recovery to a new life, in poetic form.

Kooiman, G., WHEN DEATH TAKES A FATHER, Baker Book House, 1968.

Kreis, Bernadine & Alice Pattie, UP FROM GRIEF, PATTERNS OF RECOVERY, Seabury Press, 1969.

Morse, Theresa, LIFE IS FOR LIVING, Doubleday, 1973.
> Uplifting.

*Peterson, James & Michael Brily. WIDOWS AND WIDOWHOOD, Association Press, 1977.
> Creative approach to being alone. Excellent advice.

Public Affairs Pamphlets, 381 Park Ave., S., New York 10016. "When You Lose a Loved One." 50¢. Also list of other pamphlets.

*Silverman, Phyllis, with MacKenzie, M. Pettipas & E. Wilson, HELPING EACH OTHER IN WIDOWHOOD. Health Science Publishers, 1974.
> Describes the widow-to-widow concept, evaluates organizations for widowed. Professionals add chapters on death, bereavement and grief. Bibliography.

Silverman, Phyllis, Prep. IF YOU WILL LIFT THE LOAD . . . Jewish Funeral Directors, 1976.
> Details programs that help widowed.

Start, Clarissa, WHEN YOU'RE A WIDOW, Concordia, 1968.
> Journalist describes her sudden widowhood and how she reshaped her life.

Strugnell, Cecil, ADJUSTMENT TO WIDOWHOOD AND SOME RELATED PROBLEMS, A SELECTIVE AND ANNOTATED BIBLIOGRAPHY, Health Science Publishers, 1974.

Wolf, Anna, HELPING YOUR CHILD UNDERSTAND DEATH, Child Study Press, 1973.
> Excellent discussion.

Especially for Widowers

We know of no specific books or articles, but the following might be helpful.

Dobson, Fitzhugh, HOW TO FATHER, Nash Publishing, 1974.

Farrell, Warren, THE LIBERATED MAN, Random House, 1975.
> Bibliography lists 12 articles from professional journals regarding fathers and children.

---

*Recommended.

Green, Maureen, FATHERING, McGraw-Hill, 1976.
>Discusses everything but raising children alone. Bibliography might be helpful.

Hamilton, Marshall. FATHER'S INFLUENCE ON CHILDREN, Nelson-Hall, 1977.
>Well researched by professor-author who speaks in general terms about fathering. Extensive bibliography.

Klein, Ted, THE FATHER'S BOOK, Ace Pb, 1968.
>Of general interest to fathers, but no advice for single fathers raising children.

*Levine, James, WHO WILL RAISE THE CHILDREN? Lippincott, 1976.
>Promotes the idea that fathers are as adept at childrearing as mothers.

*McFadden, Michael, BACHELOR FATHERHOOD: HOW TO RAISE AND ENJOY YOUR CHILD AS A SINGLE PARENT, Walker Publishers, Ace Pb, 1976.
>Useful, practical information for divorced fathers, but adaptable to widowers as well.

Articles

* "Let Grieving Go," *The Single Parent,* Journal of Parents Without Partners, Judith Anne Headless, October, 1975.
>Deals with the emotional aspects of loss of a mate.

* "Some Do's and Don'ts for Single Parents," Nancy Catlin, *The Single Parent,* July/August, 1974.
>Excellent practical advice for any single parent, emphasizing the crippling effects on children of pity.

* "Where Are the Neighbors Bringing in Food?", *The Single Parent,* July/August, 1974, Vidal S. Clay.
>Sensitive story about grieving by a woman who lost husbands both through death and divorce.

Resources and Groups

*Parents Without Partners, Inc., 7910 Woodmont Avenue, Washington, D.C. 20014.
>Non-profit, educational organization dedicated to single parents and their children. Over 130,000 members in nearly 900 Chapters (Spring, 1976). All ages. Conducts educational, social and family activities for members.

Widowed, Inc., 1405 Spring Rick, Houston, TX 77055.
>Model group in that city, providing crisis hotline, practical information, referral services.

THEOS (They Help Each Other Spiritually), Pittsburgh.
>Group that cooperates with other organizations (Big Brothers, Lutheran Family Services) in services to widowed. Internationally known.

Post Cana, Washington, D.C. and "Counter Foil" (for members under 40).
>A widowed group sponsored by Archdiocese which hold spiritual, intellectual and social activities.

Information Center for the Mature Woman, 515 Madison Ave., New York 10022.
>Reading lists on variety of subjects.

*Recommended.

Eschaton Club, 100 Arch St., Boston, MA. Widowed group.
> For older widowed, there are many community secular and church sponsored groups.

Parenting

Any Parent Education Group will be helpful. Many school systems, women's Commissions or PTA's sponsor parent education and single parenting groups.

YMCA's have single parent groups. They are described in *Circulator,* Vol. 6, Fall 1975. Write Mrs. Charlotte Himber, Editor, 291 Broadway, New York 10007.

Listed in the Department of Health, Education, and Welfare Booklet, "Parents Are People." No. ADM 74–48. (G.P.O. 55¢).

*American Society of Adlerian Psychology, 159 Dearborn St., Chicago, IL 60601.
> Parent education centers around the country and excellent educational materials.

*Parent Effectiveness Training Associates, 110 S. Euclid Ave., Pasadena, CA 91101.
> Parent groups in most areas.

Books

*Dreikurs, Rudolf, CHILDREN AND THE CHALLENGE, Hawthorn Books, 1974.

*Ginott, Haim, BETWEEN PARENT AND CHILD AND BETWEEN PARENT AND TEENAGER, Avon, 1965 and 1969.

*Gordon, Thomas, PARENT EFFECTIVENESS TRAINING, Peter Wyden, 1970.

*Satir, Virginia, PEOPLEMAKING, Science and Behavior, 1972.

*Walton, Francis & R. Powers, WINNING CHILDREN OVER, Practical Psychology Associates, 1974.

*Recommended.

Single Father's Reading List

*Atkin, Edith & Estelle Rubin, PART-TIME FATHER, Vanguard, 1976.
    Sensible analysis of fathering, full and part time, after divorce.

Berson, Barbara & Ben Bova, SURVIVAL GUIDE FOR THE SUDDENLY SINGLE, St. Martin's Press, 1974.
    Emphasizes divorced fathers in some Chapters.

Biller, Henry & Dennis Meredith, FATHER POWER, Anchor, 1975.
    Thorough manual for fathers who wish to participate equally with mothers in child raising. Section for single fathers.

Chew, Peter, THE INNER WORLD OF THE MIDDLE-AGED MAN, McMillan, 1976.
    Examples illustrate different aspects of life after 40.

Dobson, Fitzhugh, HOW TO FATHER, Nash Publishing Co., 1974.

*Egleson, Jim & Janet, PARENTS WITHOUT PARTNERS: GUIDE FOR DIVORCED, WIDOWED OR SEPARATED PARENTS, Dutton, 1961, Ace paperback.
    Unfortunately, this excellent book by the PWP founder is out of print.

Farrell, Warren, THE LIBERATED MAN, Random House, 1975. Bibliography has 12 listings of articles from professional journals on fathers and children.

Gilbert, Sara, WHAT'S A FATHER FOR? Warner, 1975. Practical guide to fathering in a changing world, includes part-time fathering, stepfathering.

Green, Maureen, FATHERING, McGraw-Hill, 1976.
    Discusses everything but raising children alone. Bibliography might be helpful.

Hamilton, Marshall, FATHER'S INFLUENCE ON CHILDREN, Nelson-Hall, 1977.
    Well, researched by professor-author who speaks in general terms about fathering. Extensive bibliography.

Klein, Ted. THE FATHER'S BOOK, Ace Pb, 1968.
    Of general interest to fathers, but no advice for single fathers raising children.

*Levine, James, WHO WILL RAISE THE CHILDREN? Lippincott, 1976.
    Promotes the idea that fathers are as adept at childrearing as mothers.

*McFadden, Michael, BACHELOR FATHERHOOD: HOW TO RAISE AND ENJOY YOUR CHILD AS A SINGLE PARENT, Walker Publishing Co., 1974. Ace Pb. 1976.
    Useful, practical information. The first book for custodial fathers.

*Recommended.

Metz, Charles V., DIVORCE AND CUSTODY FOR MEN, Doubleday, 1968.

> Male oriented approach to divorce and custody reform.

Stein, Edward, Ed., FATHERING, FACT OR FABLE, Abingdon, 1977.

> Collection of variety of articles, including father absence effects.

Steinzor, Bernard, WHEN PARENTS DIVORCE, New York: Pantheon, 1969.

> Fairly good advice.

Other Resources

Doppler, George F., P.O. Box 60, Broomall, PA 19008.

> Lists of Fathers' Rights Groups around the country.

*THE SINGLE PARENT, periodical of Parents Without Partners, Inc. $5.50/yr.

*PUBLIC AFFAIRS PAMPHLETS, 381 Park Avenue S., New York, NY 10016.

> Inexpensive pamphlets, many for parents and single parents.

*RMMP PUBLICATIONS, 2030 East 20th Ave., Denver, CO 80205.

> Excellent pamphlets concerning sexual responsibility: for teens.

*Reading Lists: SEPARATION AND DIVORCE (adults), and SEPARATION AND DIVORCE: ANNOTATED BIBLIOGRAPHY OF SELECTED LITERATURE FOR CHILDREN AND TEENS, and WIDOWED READING LIST. Available from Parents Without Partners, Inc., and reprinted elsewhere in this book.

*Recommended.

Epilogue

In this book you have read about some child rearing techniques that can help you in resolving family conflicts. Numerous examples have been presented that demonstrate how these techniques can be effective. Encouragement was discussed as being the "corner stone" of the relationship with your children. By stressing their assets and strengths, rather than their shortcomings, you build a very positive relationship with them.

An alternative to punishment, natural and logical consequences, was suggested. This allows you to maintain your relationship with the children even though you might be greatly upset with some of their specific behaviors. Consequences also place the responsibility for their behavior on the children themselves and, therefore, help build responsibility.

Because of the lack of communications in many single parent families, the family council was recommended. This technique allows all members to participate in family decisions and helps reduce resentment that often results when all decisions are made by the parent.

The appendix contains information that will be of interest to you. *The ABC's of Guiding the Child* on page 93 will serve as a review of the principles and techniques discussed in this book. When you feel like you need a refresher course on parenting, turn to the material in the appendix for some freshening up!

The primary theme of this book has been one of support for the single parent and confidence that families headed by single parents can be as emotionally and psychologically stable as those headed by two parents. If you are having difficulty in parenting alone, seek assistance either from helping professionals or from organizations formed to assist single parents. There are many people eager and willing to help, and remember, YOU CAN DO IT!

References

Catlin, N., Family Council, *The Single Parent*, October, 1976, pp. 19–21.

Conroy, P., *The Great Santini*, Boston: Houghton Mifflin Company, 1976.

Dinkmeyer, D., and Dreikurs, R., *Encouraging Children to Learn: The Encouragement Process*, Englewood Cliffs, N.J.: Prentice-Hall, Inc., 1963.

Dreikurs, R., and Cassel, P., *Discipline Without Tears*, New York: Hawthorn Books, Inc., 1974.

Dreikurs, R., Gould, S., and Corsini, R., *Family Council: The Dreikurs Technique*. Chicago: Henry Regnery Company, 1974.

Dreikurs, R., and Grey, L., *Logical Consequences: A New Approach to Discipline*, New York: Hawthorn Books, Inc., 1968.

Dreikurs, R., and Soltz, V., *Children: The Challenge*, New York: Hawthorn Books, Inc., 1964.

Eckstein D., Baruth, L., and Mahrer, D., *Life Style: What It Is and How to Do It*, Dubuque, Ia: Kendall/Hunt Publishing Company, 1978.

Marlin, K., *The Basics of Practical Parenting*, Columbia, MO: Practical Parenting Publication, 1973.

Reimer, C., Some Words of Encouragement, in *Study Group Leader's Manual*, edited by Vickie Soltz, Chicago: Alfred Adler Institute, 1967, pp. 71–73.

Rubin, E., The Sunday Father, *Harper's Bazaar*, July, 1976, pp. 47 and 90.

Spencer, H., *Education—Intellectual, Moral, Physical*, New York: P.D. Alden Publishers, 1885.

Appendix

The ABC's of Guiding the Child

Rudolf Dreikurs, M.D.—Margaret Goldman[1]

1. Reprinted by permission of the Rudolf Dreikurs Unit of the Family Education Association, Chicago, Illinois. Separate copies of *The ABC's of Guiding the Child* are available by writing the Family Education Association, c/o Gene Hankin, 821 LaCrosse Ct., Wilmette, Illinois 60091.

GOLDEN RULE: "Do unto others as you would have others do unto you." This is the basis of democracy, since it implies equality of individuals.

RESPECT, based upon the assumption of equality, is the inalienable right of all human beings. No one should take advantage of another; neither adult nor child should be a slave or tyrant. Adults have an unrecognized prejudice against children, which prevents them from really respecting the child. When parents show respect for the child—while winning his respect for them—teach the child to respect himself and others.

ENCOURAGEMENT implies faith in and respect for the child as he is. Don't discourage the child by having too high standards and being overambitious for him. A child misbehaves only when he is discouraged and believes he cannot succeed by useful means. A child needs encouragement as a plant needs sunshine and water. When we tell a child he could be better we are really saying he is not good enough as he is.

CHILDREN WHO "DON'T CARE" ARE DISPLAYING A FACADE OF COURAGE—BRAVADO. Many children who seemingly don't care what happens are discouraged about their ability to do what is required. To protect themselves from constant recriminations and punishment, they "don't care" what others think or do. They believe they no longer are able to act properly. Every child wants basically to belong and be accepted in his environment.

FEELINGS OF "SECURITY" are purely subjective and not necessarily related to the actual situation. Security cannot be found from the outside; it is only possible through the feeling of strength. A child, to feel secure, needs:

> Courage— "I'm willing to take a chance."
> Confidence— "I'll be able to handle it."
> Optimism— "Things will turn out all right."

Obviously, parents can do much toward influencing children in these directions by setting examples of courage, confidence, and optimism in their daily lives. Courage is as contagious as anxiety.

REWARD AND PUNISHMENT are outdated. A child soon considers a reward his right and demands a reward for everything. He considers that punishment gives him the right to punish in turn, and the retaliation of children is usually more effective than the punishment inflicted by the parents. Children often retaliate by not eating, fighting, neglecting schoolwork, or otherwise misbehaving in ways that are the most disturbing to the parents.

NATURAL AND LOGICAL CONSEQUENCES are techniques which allow the child to experience the actual result of his own behavior.

Natural consequences are the direct result of the child's behavior. For example: A child is careless, falls down, hurts his knee. Next time he will be more careful.

Logical consequences are established by the parents, and are a direct and logical—not arbitrarily imposed—consequence of the transgression. For example: A child is late for dinner. Instead of reminding or punishing, mother has quietly removed his plate. Regardless of his reaction, parents maintain a friendly attitude, based on the assumption that the child was not hungry enough to come when dinner was served.

In both instances the parent allows the child to experience the consequences of his own actions, instead of using personal authority through reminding and punishing. Through these techniques the child is motivated toward proper behavior through his personal experience of the social order in which he lives. Only in moments of real danger is it necessary to protect the child from the consequences of his disturbing behavior.

Natural consequences are always effective. Logical consequences can only be applied if there is no power contest otherwise they degenerate into punitive retaliation.

ACTING INSTEAD OF TALKING is more effective in conflict situations. Talking provides an opportunity for arguments in which the child can defeat the parent. Children tend to become "mother deaf" and will act only when punishment is threatened. Usually a child knows very well what is expected of him. Never explain to a child what he already knows and has heard repeatedly. Talking should be restricted to friendly conversations and should not be used as a disciplinary means. For example: If you are driving your car and your children start to quarrel and fight, instead of telling them to be quiet, the parent can pull the car to the curb and simply wait for them to be quiet. If the parent maintains a calm, patient attitude, he can, through quiet action accomplish positive results.

WITHDRAWAL AS AN EFFECTIVE COUNTERACTION: Withdrawal (leaving the child and walking into another room) is most effective when the child demands undue attention or tries to involve you in a power contest. He gets no satisfaction in annoying if nobody pays attention, nor will his tantrums work without an audience. Withdrawal is not surrender nor indifference. Beware of overconcern: feeling you must "do something" about every situation. Often doing nothing effects wonderful results.

WITHDRAW FROM THE PROVOCATION BUT NOT FROM THE CHILD. Don't talk in moments of conflict. Give attention and recognition when children behave well, but not when they demand it with disturbing behavior. At these times attention becomes a premium for bad behavior. The less attention the child gets when he disturbs, the more he needs when he is cooperative. You may feel that anger helps you rid of your own tensions, but it does not teach the child what you think he should learn.

DISTINGUISH BETWEEN POSITIVE AND NEGATIVE ATTENTION if you want to influence children's behavior. Positive attention is any action toward the child that is basically friendly. Negative attention is any action that is basically unfriendly (annoyance, anger, and the resulting scolding, punishment—see Goals). Children who are discouraged about their ability to behave properly will misbehave in order to gain parent's attention—even though it is negative attention. Feeling unable to gain positive attention, and regarding indifference as intolerable, children resort to activities which get them negative attention. Negative attention is the evidence that they have succeeded in accomplishing their goal.

CHILDREN KNOW WHAT'S RIGHT AND WRONG, but the knowledge doesn't prevent them from doing what is wrong. If the child gains benefits (negative attention) from his wrong behavior, he will continue it. Parents find it difficult to understand that children regard negative attention as a benefit. Consequently they resort to preaching right and wrong to a child who is well aware of the difference.

WE MUST SEE THE PURPOSE OF A LIE instead of regarding it merely as "bad." Lying, like all human behavior, serves a purpose. Children may lie to avoid punishment, to make themselves feel important, to defy the parents, etc. Most parents condemn and punish children for lying, feeling morally outraged, thereby giving the child the satisfaction which he sought in lying. Unless the parent becomes aware of the function of the lie, he can do nothing about it. Preaching is ineffectual and may ultimately convince the child that he is a "liar" and a "bad" person.

DON'T INTERFERE IN CHILDREN'S FIGHTS. By allowing children to resolve their own conflicts they learn to get along better. Many fights are provoked to get the parent involved, and by separating the children or acting as judge we fall for their provocation, thereby stimulating them to fight more.

FIGHTS REQUIRE COOPERATION. We tend to consider cooperation as inherent in a positive relationship only. When children fight they are also cooperating in a mutual endeavor. If one does not wish to continue, the fight stops. When parents learn this, they will discontinue punishing the "culprit" and dispensing sympathy to the "victim." Often the younger, weaker child provokes a fight so the parents will act against the older child. When two children fight, they are both participating and are equally responsible.

TAKE TIME FOR TRAINING and teaching the child essential skills and habits. Don't attempt to train a child in a moment of conflict or in company. Allow for training at calm times, regularly, until the lesson is learned. If many areas need improvement, give attention to one at a time. Limit yourself to what you can do. The mother who "does not have time" for such training will have to spend more time correcting an untrained child.

LIMIT YOURSELF TO WHAT YOU CAN DO. When many areas of conflict exist, parents try to correct everything at once. In attempting such an impossible task, they generally threaten or warn children of future punishment or consequences. Often such statements are meaningless since the parent discovers he cannot enforce his words. Parents will have more success with their children if they limit their discipline to areas in which they can enforce rules merely by being firm. For example: If you are unable to keep a child indoors, don't insist that he stay in.

AVOID LETTING YOUR OWN NEED FOR PRESTIGE influence you in training your child. For example: If your child knows how to dress but is sloppy about his personal appearance, avoid the impulse to remind him or straighten his clothes yourself because you are afraid of what others will think of you as a mother. Your own prestige is less important than letting the child learn for himself.

GREAT EXPECTATIONS OFTEN PRODUCE LITTLE RESULTS. First distinguish between great expectations and realistic expectations. Once a child has learned to tie his shoes, he is always expected to tie them. This is a realistic expectation based on the child's demonstrated ability. Great, or high expectations are based primarily on the parents' desire for excellence in their children. Ambitious, competitive parents demonstrate to their children their high expectations through exacting demands and pressures to "do better." Parental ambitions for children concern any quality the parents deem important; i.e., intellectual achievement, popularily, artistic skill, masculinity, ad infinitum. Such parents want their children to be the best in the area of the parents' choosing. Parents with bright children usually comment, "you could do better if you tried," which is tantamount to, "you are not good enough the way you are." Remarks of this nature coupled with parental pressures are usually discouraging in the child who then produces little or no achievement.

COMPETITION MEANS "I give up where you succeed—I move into areas where you fail." Each child wants an individual place and recognition in his family. If brother or sister has established an area of success in ability or personality, the other sibling will differ in an attempt to be unique, feeling unable to attain the success of the other. For example: If the first child excels in school work, the second, feeling discouraged about his ability to "be as good as his sibling" may give up in that area and become disinterested in school work. Or, if one child is very popular the next may be more interested in solitary activities. If one child is not pleasant, the next may be utterly charming, etc. Parents help to establish an atmosphere of competition—the more competitive and ambitious they are, the more their children will differ.

NEVER DO FOR A CHILD WHAT HE CAN DO FOR HIMSELF. A "dependent" child is a demanding child. Maintain order and establish your own independence. Most adults underestimate the abilities of children. Give children opportunities and encouragement to become contributing members of the family and other groups. Children become irresponsible only when we fail to give them opportunities to take on responsibility. In assuming the child's responsibility we deprive him of the opportunity to learn. Don't indulge yourself by giving service.

OVERPROTECTION PUSHES A CHILD DOWN. When mother gives services to a child who is able to do things for himself, she is saying in effect, "You are too small, too lacking in ability, too lacking in judgment—you are inferior." Mothers may feel they are giving when they act for a child, actually they are taking away the child's right to learn and develop. Parents have an unrecognized prejudice against children; they assume children are incapable of acting responsibly. When parents begin to have faith that their children can behave in a responsible way, while allowing them to do so, the children will assume their own responsibilities.

OVER-RESPONSIBLE PARENTS OFTEN PRODUCE IRRESPON-SIBLE CHILDREN. Parents who take on the responsibility of the child by reminding or doing for him encourage the child to be irresponsible. The child quickly learns that he doesn't have to remember for himself—mother will remember for him. He also learns that he does not have to do things for himself—eventually mother will do them for him. A child who always "forgets" usually has a mother who always remembers. Parents must learn to "mind their own business" and let the child learn from the logical consequences of his own behavior.

PARENTS' DEPENDENCE ON THE CHILD is a difficult concept to recognize. In many instances a mother who constantly reminds and does things for a child unnecessarily not only takes the child's responsibility away from him, but also becomes dependent on him for her feelings of importance as a mother. Often mothers will feel useless in the home unless they keep themselves constantly busy with the child.

"GOOD" MOTHERS ARE AMERICA'S TRAGEDY. They feel worthless if their children are not perfect. In their determination to achieve this ambition, they correct every deficiency and give continuous service, often raising children who become deficient and irresponsible. "Goodness" walks hand-in-hand with "superiority," often neither husband nor children have a chance in life with such a "superior" mother. A "good" mother always "knows best" is always "right"!

CHILDREN ARE GOOD OBSERVERS BUT POOR INTERPRETERS. Children are able to observe activities accurately, but often draw incorrect conclusions from them. Examples: When a new baby arrives, mother necessarily pays a great deal of attention to it. The older child sees and interprets this to mean that mother loves baby more than him. He equates attention and love. Or, a child who is pampered greatly may conclude that he is a helpless baby. He observes how his parents treat each other, and wrongly concludes that all men and women behave this way. His observations are keen, his interpretations often faulty. It is the faulty interpretation that remains with him throughout his life, coloring all his behavior.

UNDERSTAND THE CHILD'S GOAL. Every action of a child has a purpose. His basic aim is to have him place in the group. A well-adjusted child has found his way toward social acceptance by conforming with the requirements of the group and by making his own useful contribution to it. The misbehaving child is still trying, in a mistaken way, to feel important in his own world. For example: a young child who has never been allowed to dress himself (because "mother is in a hurry") who has not been allowed to help in the house ("you're not big enough to set the table"), will lack the feeling that he is a useful, contributing member of the family, and will feel important only when arousing mother's anger and annoyance with his misbehavior.

THE FOUR GOALS OF A CHILD'S MISBEHAVIOR. The child is usually unaware of his goals. His behavior, though illogical to others, is consistent with his own interpretation of his place in the family group.

GOAL 1: Attention-getting—he wants attention and service.
GOAL 2: Power—he wants to be the boss.
GOAL 3: Revenge—he wants to hurt us.
GOAL 4: Display of inadequacy—he wants to be left alone, with no demands made upon him.

OUR REACTIONS TO A CHILD'S MISBEHAVIOR PATTERNS. Very often we can discover a child's goals by observing our own reactions to his behavior. For example:

When his goal is Attention-getting, we respond by feeling annoyed and that we need to remind and coax him.

When his goal is Power, we respond by feeling provoked and get into a power contest with him— "You can't get away with this!"

When his goal is Revenge, we respond by feeling deeply hurt and "I'll get even!"

When his goal is Display of Inadequacy, we respond by feeling despair and "I don't know what to do!"

If your first impulse is to react to one of these four ways, you can be fairly sure you have discovered the goal of the child's misbehavior.

A CHILD WHO WANTS TO BE POWERFUL, generally has a parent who also seeks power. If mother insists on her own way, the child imitates her and they become involved in a power contest. Each feels honor-bound to do just the opposite of what is asked. The harder parents try to "control" their children, the less success they will have. One person cannot fight alone; when mother learns to do nothing (by withdrawing, etc.) during a power contest, she dissipates the child's power, and can begin to establish a healthier relationship with him. The use of power teaches children only that strong people get what they want.

BEHAVIOR IS MOVEMENT. No person behaves without intending to affect others. One is usually not aware of the purpose of one's own behavior, if this purpose is not reconcilable with one's conscience, and with the assumed good intentions which we all have and display.

To understand the child's pattern of movement through life, one must become sensitive to the inter-actions inherent in routine situations. For example: Assume a child dawdles every morning and "forgets" to do most things that are rightfully his responsibility. Mother responds with constant reminders and doing many things for him. At school, teacher has to remind and push to make him work. What is the inter-relationship? Actually the child is, through his behavior, provoking others to assume his responsibilities. This behavior, then, may become a permanent pattern, a way of moving through life.

DON'T ACT ON YOUR FIRST IMPULSE. By acting on your first impulse you tend to intensify the child's misbehavior patterns rather than correct them. You act in accordance with his expectations and thereby fortify his mistaken goals. What can you do if you don't know what to do? First, think of what you know would be wrong to do and refrain from doing it; the rest is usually all right. Second, imagine what the child expects you to do, and then do the opposite. That throws the child off guard, and then you can arrange with him a mutual solution to the situation.

NO HABIT IS MAINTAINED if it loses its purpose, loses its benefits. Children tend to develop "bad" habits when they derive the benefit of negative attention. Example: A child occasionally picks his nose. Mother finds it unpleasant, and tells him not to do it. The child quickly learns that this is a good way to upset mother, so he continues it. Without realizing the dynamics of the situation, mother inadvertently encourages the habit.

MINIMIZE MISTAKES. Making mistakes is human. Regard your mistakes as inevitable instead of feeling guilty, and you'll learn better. We must have the courage to be imperfect. The child is also imperfect. Don't make too much fuss and don't worry about his mistakes. Build on the positive, not on the negative. For example: Instead of pointing out how poorly he ties his shoes, point out instead how well he can button his shirt.

MAKING MISTAKES LOWERS STATUS. The more mistakes we make the lower we are on the ladder of success, and vice versa. We forget that learning occurs through making mistakes. A child who fears making mistakes will only make more; such a child loses his spontaneity and creativity in life. Ambition to live up to parental high standards (no mistakes) often undermines the child's trust in his own ability. Parents need the courage to be imperfect, for themselves, and as an example for their children. Perfection implies a finality which does not fit into life, and allows no room for life's unfolding.

DON'T BE CONCERNED WITH WHAT OTHERS DO, but accept responsibility for what you can do. By utilizing the full potential of your own constructive influence, you do not have to think about what others should do to the child. Compensation for the mistakes of others is unwise, and over-protection may rob the child of his own courage and resourcefulness. For example: If father is too harsh with the child, the mother runs to protect, three negative results are accomplished. First, mother deprives father and child from learning to get along with each other. Second, mother teaches the child to run to her for protection instead of using his own resources. Third, mother antagonizes the father so that he is less willing to cooperate with her in dealing with the child.

A FAMILY COUNCIL gives every member of the family a chance to express herself freely in all matters of both difficulty and pleasure pertaining to the family as a whole, and to participate in the responsibilities each member of the family has for the welfare of all. It is truly education for democracy and should not become a place for parents to "preach" or impose their will on children, nor should it deteriorate into a "gripe" session. The emphasis should be on "What we can do about the situation." Meet regularly at the same time each week. Rotate chairman. Keep minutes. Have an equal vote for each member. Let any poor decisions stand until the following week.

SHOW SYMPATHY TO A CHILD, BUT DON'T FEEL SORRY FOR HIM. When you feel sorry for him, the child feels justified in feeling sorry for himself and begins to believe that life owes him something. There is no one so miserable as the person who feels sorry for himself. Actual physical damage (polio disability, etc.) will harm a child much less than the pitying attitudes of parents and relatives. Children have tremendous resiliency and courage to go on. Feeling sorry for them robs them of their courage and adds to their suffering.

HAVE FUN TOGETHER and thereby help to develop a relationship based on mutual respect, love and affection, mutual confidence and trust, and a feeling of belonging. Playing together, working together, sharing interesting and exciting experiences lead to the kind of closeness which is essential for cooperation. Instead of talking to nag, scold, preach and correct, utilize talking to maintain a friendly relationship. Speak to your child as you would speak to your friend.